Easy
Bread
Machine
Recipes

Rob Wanless

Sterling Publishing Co., Inc.
New York

D0176217

Dedicated to Ada Lai and Marianne Wright

The following recipes previously appeared in *Best Breads: Any Way You Slice It* by Rob Wanless, published by the American Cooking Guild in 1994. They are reprinted by permission: Basic Bread, Dill Bread, Orangiest Orange Bread, Sandwich Rolls, English Muffins, Hot Cross Buns, Hawaiian Pizza, and Pizza Dough.

Library of Congress Cataloging-in-Publication Data

Wanless, Rob.
     Easy bread machine recipes / Rob Wanless.
       p.   cm.
     Includes index.
     ISBN 0-8069-9700-1
     1. Bread. Automatic bread machines. I. Title.
  TX769.W284   1997
  641.8'15—dc21   96-48697
                                      CIP

10 9 8 7 6 5

Published by Sterling Publishing Company, Inc.
387 Park Avenue South, New York, N.Y. 10016
© 1997 by Rob Wanless
Distributed in Canada by Sterling Publishing
c/o Canadian Manda Group, One Atlantic Avenue, Suite 105
Toronto, Ontario, Canada M6K 3E7
Distributed in Great Britain and Europe by Cassell PLC
Wellington House, 125 Strand, London WC2R 0BB, England
Distributed in Australia by Capricorn Link (Australia) Pty Ltd.
P.O. Box 6651, Baulkham Hills, Business Centre, NSW 2153, Australia
Manufactured in the United States of America
All rights reserved

Sterling ISBN 0-8069-9700-1

Contents

Preface

With about 30 bread machine cookbooks out there, why buy this one? Those other books run the gamut from simple recipe books all the way to one that purports to be "the ultimate." Some of them are very good, some are fairly good but look great, and so on. But all of them—except this one, of course—are superfluous. After you use this book, you won't need a bread machine cookbook at all.

You don't have a bread machine? Well, if you don't have a bread machine, and you like bread—get one! If you don't have a bread machine, and don't intend to get one, then this book may not be for you—unless you just like to collect cookbooks—and that's okay.

This book is about baking bread in—or making dough for other goodies with—a bread machine. And that ranges from just plain bread to fancy dinner rolls, English muffins, braided loaves, round loaves, and pizza dough. You know, real bakery stuff.

So, if you're standing in the bookstore reading this, you might just as well go ahead and buy it, because this book is different. First of all, my recipes are easier to follow than most, probably because I like to explain everything simply. Second, my recipes are very good. This is because I like to eat well and I have good taste. And third: my recipes work. In fact, they work better in a couple of bread machines than the recipes that come with the machines do.

But the main reason this book is different is because I show how you can get away *without using recipes at all.* You do use the recipes in your head, of course, but the truth is, to make bread, all you need to do is keep the basic proportions in mind. These are 2½ parts dry to 1 part wet ingredients (more or less; with bread, it is always going to be "more or less").

In this book I'm going to show you why it is unnecessary to spend extra money on those "bread mixes" to use in the bread machine. Bread mixes, indeed! Flour and water are all you really need.

Here is how you make bread. You take 1 cup of water, 2½ cups of flour, 1 tsp of salt, and 1 tsp of yeast and put those four ingredients into your bread machine, in the order the owner's manual advises; you press the start button, and in a few hours you'll have a wonderful, nutritious, delicious loaf of bread. That's right, you don't need sugar or shortening.

I've included about a hundred recipes, all of which are wonderful, and all of them will get you started making your own stuff. These recipes are not for a bunch of "health breads" that are nutritious as hell, taste funny, and are hard to digest. I give you recipes for, and teach you how to make, real honest-to-goodness tasty breads—like Vienna Bread, Parker House Rolls, Hot Cross Buns, and a Swiss Christmas loaf so rich and good just reading the recipe will put 2½ pounds on you. Included are our own adaptations of challah, sourdough rye, pizza, real French bread, and English muffins, as well as Holly's incredible Tuscan Tailgate Loaf, developed for a tailgate party. She wrapped it in aluminum foil and put it next to the exhaust manifold of our car's engine (it's an Italian car, of course) to keep warm. She has also developed a cheese Danish so good it almost defies natural law.

Using this book, you'll soon think as we do at our house: *if it's in the kitchen, it can go in the bread machine.* This book will help you overcome any fear of making something unusual in your machine. If you mess up, you can always use the results as a doorstop or throw them out, or even at, someone.

There are a few things you should know about us (it is an "us"—my wife, Holly, being the other party). Neither of us is a "food professional," as they say in the food trade; we're not food engineers or nutritionists. We are a man and wife who have been cooking for a combined total of over 70 years. We have raised a large family, and if you're not rich and like to eat good food, that means one whole lot of cooking. We don't necessarily love to cook (I mean for the *art* of cooking) but we do love to eat—and eat well. Holly is the daughter of a chef, Fred Crissman, who spent nearly 50 years cooking professionally, and at 85 can still outcook all of us. I was raised in what now would be called a gourmet grocery store, Ginocchio's, in Palm Beach, Florida, back when Palm Beach was really snobby. Then all the "big houses" had at least a couple of cooks. My aunt Selina would say things like: "Here, this is good, taste this!" And I would be treated to some glorious concoction of hers, or from one of the estates that her store served. The result was that even though I wasn't born with a silver spoon in my mouth, the one that was in there had caviar, or at least a good *foie gras,* on it. So my wife and I both learned about good food early, and "as the twig is bent," so they say.

We have both been blessed with good health. We try to maintain this gift with our diet: we eat in moderation what is in season and avoid diet fads and the latest fears about what is killing off our fellows and presently causing cancer in laboratory rats. (We, by the way, didn't fall for the great egg scare.) We buy very few prepared foods, and that, it should go without saying, includes bread.

We bake our own bread and rolls because they're better than we can buy, and it was fairly easy to do, even before there were bread machines. Over the years I've tried to match the Italian bread our neighbor brought us from New York, the rye bread from Greenberg's in Philadelphia, and the wonderful breads and rolls I remember from the Palm Beach Pastry Shoppe, 40-some years ago. I have also worked on a marvelous sourdough bread as I remembered it from San Francisco—when I lived there in the early 1960s. I actually got pretty close to duplicating that bread.

We are not kitchen gadget freaks. When we bought our first bread machine 5 years ago, it was not because it was the coming thing, but to save time. The bread machine helped provide excellent breads and rolls we were used to, with nowhere near as much time being spent on them. And it saved us money. It paid for itself in the first nine months. We paid a little over $200 for the first model Panasonic produced. We used the machine practically every day, averaging over 5 loaves or batches of rolls a week at around 40¢ each, for a net saving of about $4 or $5 a week. But saving money is no big thing if your bread and rolls taste awful and have no nutritional value.

The recipes which came with the machine seemed pretty good at first, and produced better than what we could buy at the store. But we were soon developing our own recipes, drawing not only from our own bread baking experience but from the dozens of books on bread baking we had read over the years. Bread is easy to make, and with the bread machine it's even easier. With a bread machine you can have high-quality bread and rolls routinely, which otherwise requires either a lot of work and planning or a very good baker nearby. The bread machine saved money in other ways: no more running out to get a loaf of bread or pack of rolls at the last minute, ending up getting a half-dozen things you really don't need.

Our recipes haven't been developed and tested in antiseptic, shiny, stainless steel, climate-controlled, professional kitchens—ones that bear little resemblance to yours or ours. They've been tested by us, our daughters, Lydia and Kirsten, and our neighbors and friends. These recipes have been developed in our kitchen, in our own bread machines, by us. In testing the recipes, we have made it a point to use ingredients off the shelves of local grocery stores, just like the ones you buy. There are a few exceptions, like yeast, which we buy inexpensively in 1-pound packs. (So can you; we'll go into that in the Ingredients section of the book.)

You'll find recipes are for the three common sizes of bread machines—the 1 pound, 1½ pound, and 2 pound size. Some recipes are designed to be baked in the machine, and some are designed to have the dough prepared in the machine, with the baking done in the oven. The recipes work in all the leading brands presently sold—Breadman, Panasonic, Welbilt, Maxim, Mr. Loaf, Hitachi, Toastmaster, West Bend, and Zojirushi, to name a few.

So if you're still standing in the store reading this, go pay for it, take it home, and let's get down to some serious bread making.

Introduction

First, get to know your bread machine. Read the owner's manual which came with your machine. Find out whether your machine has a yeast dispenser. This can determine the order in which the ingredients are put in the machine. Some bread machines come with a "fruit beeper," which tells you when to add fruit and nuts during the dough-making cycle. When you use my recipes, follow the basic guidelines and directions in the manual for your machine, adding the yeast as your machine's instructions direct you to.

By now, you've probably baked a couple of loaves using some of the recipes that came with the machine. They aren't bad—actually they're pretty good. They probably seem sensational if the only bread you've been eating is store-bought.

Several of the better machines suggest you might have to add a little more or less water or flour as you adapt the type of ingredients you use to your machine or your climate. They usually suggest this right after they tell you to measure everything accurately. This may appear to be a contradiction, but it isn't. You'll soon understand the effects of the climate, season, humidity or dryness of the air, altitude, etc. All these things can and probably will affect your bread. Don't panic. Usually the differences are only small ones. If you live in an area with heavy fog or rain, you'll probably want to add a bit more flour to the ingredients given. In cold weather, you'll want to warm the water and other ingredients before putting them in the machine. If you live at a high altitude, you'll need a little less yeast. Some of the owner's manuals will give you tips about these sorts of things.

The recipes that come with the machines are similar almost to the point of being identical. For that matter, the recipes for most breads are similar. The differences in the recipes reflect the tastes of the preparers. Most differences are not in the basic ingredients, but in the various goodies different cooks stick in the breads, and in the techniques they've developed.

You might want to go to the library and check out a few books on bread making. Try Judith Olney's *Judith Olney on Bread* (Crown, 1985); it's one of my favorites. James Beard's *Beard on Bread* (Knopf, 1973) is another, and Bernard Clayton's books on the breads of France, for example, *The Breads of France* (Bobbs-Merrill, 1978), are great. But you don't have to do that to make good bread with your little bread machine. This little book and a love of good bread are all you need.

The bread machine is your tool to help you to have baked goods above the ordinary—without the time and work. If you are the normal overworked cook, you will be perfectly happy just tossing ingredients into the bread pan of your machine and enjoying the results. The bread machine takes care of any possible drudgery or mystery of bread making for you. It mixes the flour, water, salt, and yeast, tasks people have had to do by hand for several thousand years. The bread machine deals with the mysteries of kneading the dough, letting it rise, punching it down. Then, cooperative thing that it is, it even bakes the bread for you. All you have to do is toss in the ingredients, select what you want, when you want it, and push a button. That's all there is to it. *O brave new world, that has such wonders in it!*

There is nothing that starts the morning off like awakening to the smell of freshly baked bread. The timer makes that possible, without your having to get up at dawn to start your baking. We deliberately have not said whether or not you can use a particular recipe with the timer. Use your common sense when deciding this. If you are using a recipe that calls for fruit and nuts, they should be added towards the end of the kneading cycle, so that the machine doesn't chew up the nuts and raisins during the kneading. That means you need to be around to add them. Some machines have a beeper indicating when to add fruit or nuts. Otherwise, you can calculate the length of the kneading cycle and add the fruit and nuts 5 minutes before the end. For this reason, these recipes are best done without the timer.

Some books say you shouldn't use milk in baking with the timer, because it might spoil while remaining in the machine for several hours uncooked. If you want hot bread tomorrow morning or when you come home from work, use the timer, but if you're a little squeamish about milk being left unrefrigerated, stick with those recipes that use dry milk when the ingredients will be unrefrigerated for several hours before baking.

THE ORGANIZATION OF THE BOOK

We have divided the book into several sections. In the Ingredients chapter, we try to answer most of the questions you're likely to have about what you can put into your machine. Next comes Easy Recipes for Getting Started, a few basic bread recipes.

Then we get to the other reason for the book: the recipes. We've divided them into two sections based on the principal ways of using bread machines: The first is Recipes for the Bake Setting, for the breads mixed, kneaded, risen, and baked in the machine. The breads in the bake setting section are divided into Basic Breads, Dark Breads (whole wheats, ryes, and whole grains), Savory Breads, Fruit Breads, and Miscellanous Breads that don't fit in the other categories.

The second main section of the book is Oven-Baked Creations, for recipes that are kneaded and have the first rise in the bread machine but are hand-finished by you and baked in an oven. This section shows the versatility of the bread machines. They take care of the time-consuming first steps in the baking process, giving you a nicely kneaded lump of dough, ready to work into those great bakery products which, unless you live in a city blessed with a really good bakery, you probably can't find anymore. We start off with a short review of kneading and raising dough, in case you haven't done this before. The Oven-Baked Creations continues with Oven-Baked Breads, including those breads that must be finished by hand and baked in a conventional oven, such as braided challah, long French loaves, and Italian and Vienna loaves. Another section gives you Oven-Baked Sweet Loaves, including Raisin Breads. Then there are the Rolls and Breadsticks, including Sandwich Rolls and my wonderful Parker House Rolls, Bagels, English Muffins, Croissants, and more. There are sections of Oven-Baked Creations on Sweet Rolls, and on Holiday Breads and Rolls, including breakfast treats and specialty breads, and finally, to give you a further idea of the versatility of the machine, we include a couple of meals from your bread machine.

There are also chapters about bread machines and alternate bread machines, such as food processors and blenders, which you can read if you're planning on buying a new machine, and some ideas about what to do with leftover bread. So, let's get on with it!

Ingredients and Tools

In this book, most measurements are by volume rather than weight. This includes flour, shortening, and water. US liquid measure units are used, in which 1 cup (C) is 8 fluid ounces. One tablespoon (T) is three teaspoons (tsp). Let's start with a review: the basic ingredients of bread are flour, water, salt and yeast. That's all it takes to make bread. (Of course, that's not all you can put in bread.)

Yeast

The first ingredient, which is least in quantity but absolutely essential to make the bread rise, is yeast. Yeast is a fungus. (Let me call it a tiny living thing. That sounds better.) People have known of yeast since ancient times. It is and has been an important ingredient in beer and numerous other important beverages, and the principal leaven of bread for at least 5000 years. Yeast grows, and rather quickly, but to do so it must feed on something, like sugar. It can feed on the sugar found in the flour, or on sugar added to it. As it grows, it turns sugar into alcohol. (Is that beginning to sound like beer? The eminent French baker Pierre Poulain calls good bread "baked beer.") This process makes a gas, carbon dioxide. When you make dough from wheat flour, you work the flour, or knead it, to make fibers from something in the flour called gluten. These fibers that form trap the carbon dioxide gas as it expands; that's what makes bread rise. Yeast is everywhere, in the air we breathe, etc. For centuries it was bought in cakes, or was allowed to develop and grow naturally in a starter. The development and perfecting of dry yeast made the bread machine possible.

For the bread machine, you need active dry yeast, not the yeast that is sold in blocks or cakes. My recipes use active dry yeast that is designed to rise rapidly. If you use regular active dry yeast, increase the amount of yeast you use by 25%. Yeast freezes well, so we keep a small jar of it in the refrigerator and the rest in an airtight container in the freezer. Don't buy those little three-envelope packs. They are too expensive for bread machine users. Four-ounce jars are a bit better, but are still expensive if you calculate the per-pound cost. Buy your yeast by the pound. Look for it in a store featuring bulk items. You should be able to find it in 1- or 2-pound packs or blocks.

A pound lasts us about 3 months—and we bake almost every day. Even if, or when, the yeast starts to lose its oomph, after two months or so, and you have to toss it, you still save lots of money by buying it in bulk.

If you have had no experience with making bread, yeast may spook you. You may have heard of proofing (activating the yeast by mixing it with water), killing the yeast, and the like. Well, with the bread machine, you don't even have to think about yeast, except to remember to add it in the recommended quantity, according to the directions.

You either mix the yeast in with the other dry ingredients or add it automatically from a yeast dispenser, depending upon the type of bread machine you have. Read the instructions which came with your bread machine to find out how yours works, and follow the suggested method of adding yeast when using the recipes in this book.

Flour

After yeast, the next most important ingredient is, of course, flour—wheat flour, to be specific. Of course, there are as many kinds of flour as there are grains from which to grind it, and we'll touch on some of those in a moment. But for the vast majority of us, wheat flour, either white or whole wheat, is the preferred.

Wheat flour comes in four "strengths." Cake, which is very soft, is used for cakes. Pastry, not quite as soft, is good for pie crusts and pancakes, waffles and the like. Then there are the two we use most: all-purpose and, the strongest of all, bread flour. Strength is determined by the quantity of gluten in the flour, which is determined by the hardness of the wheat.

We won't discuss the first two flours, cake and pastry flour, except to say you don't want to use either in your bread machine—unless your machine makes cakes. (We don't have recipes for cakes in this book, however.)

In the US, our flour supply is usually wonderful. So, if you ever run short of things to give thanks for when you're saying your prayers, just think about flour, and the fact that the US produces enough to feed many people all around the world.

You may notice some flours labeled "stone ground." Stone-ground flours get ground at temperatures that are lower than flours ground by steel rollers, so fewer of their nutrients and flavors are lost.

A bag of all-purpose flour, unopened, will have a shelf life of a year or more if stored in a cool, dry place. This varies from brand to brand, so check with the manufacturer if you want specifics. Refrigerate the flour in the seasons when it is hot in your area. Whole wheat flour, or any whole-grain flour, which has some fat in it, can go rancid, so store it in the refrigerator unless you're using it in a month or two. For long-term storage, you can wrap flours in moisture-proof covers and store them in the freezer.

ALL-PURPOSE FLOUR

Most of the time, all we use is good old, all-purpose flour. All-purpose flour comes two ways: bleached and unbleached. It is about 10 to 11% protein.

Judith Olney, in her wonderful book on breads, says she prefers unbleached all-purpose flour to bread flour—it has fewer chemicals, and it is hard to tell the difference in the final product. We had two bread machines a few years ago. In one we could use unbleached all-purpose flour just fine; in the other one, the loaves were a bit lower and not as fine-textured.

In preparing this book we've noticed the manuals from some of the newer machines only mention all-purpose flour. We aren't radicals about chemicals and preservatives, but we would just as soon avoid them when we can. Then there is this: bread flour is really expensive. It costs half again as much as all-purpose flour.

In our area, 25- or or 50-pound bags of flour don't seem as good a buy as the 5-pound ones in the grocery stores. Most chain stores offer a pretty good store brand, which is probably just one of the brand-name flours packaged in the store wrapper. There are several high-quality flours available, in which there is a difference, and there should be, since they cost twice what the other brands cost. But they are good to use when saving money isn't a priority and come holiday time when you want everything to be a little special.

The first two brands that come to mind are King Arthur and Hodgson Mills. Both good flours. But I've checked around and have found something special: There is a brand of flour sold mainly in the southern United States, White Lily. I first read about in an article in *Gourmet* magazine about a restaurant in Charleston noted for its biscuits. The lady who was explaining how to make them said, "Don't even try to make them without White Lily self-rising flour." This is the flour Southern women will fight like hell to defend. Use it and you'll see why. I picked some up while visiting our son in Fayetteville. The women are right. (White Lily now offers a bread flour the equal to their self-rising white flour, and it is now available outside the South by mail order.)

If you don't think your bread is rising high enough using unbleached all-purpose flour, you can always add high-gluten flour or gluten to it.

BREAD FLOUR

Bread flour has more gluten than all-purpose flour and a higher protein content, 14 to 18 grams per cup, or about 12.5%. In the US, it's milled from the hard wheats grown in the Dakotas, northern Texas, and other inhospitable climes. Some malted barley is added to bread flour to promote yeast fermentation. Bread flour is more granular than all-purpose flour and works with yeast better than the other flours do. This helps to produce nice high loaves of bread. Bread flour also comes bleached, presifted, enriched, and bromated. (*Bromated* means they've added chemicals to help the yeast work better, which affects the crumb and crust.) Bread flour, by the way, doesn't work well for baking things other than bread. If you're only going to keep two kinds of flour, stick with the all-purpose and pastry.

HIGH-GLUTEN FLOUR

High-gluten flour is about 14% protein. Recently, one of our neighbors gave us a 25-lb bag of professional baker's high-gluten flour. We mixed some of this flour with the other flours. This added strength and helped the other flours to rise better. One example of high-gluten flour is General Mills All Trumps Flour. In recipes that have other flours that are low in gluten, such as rye or cornmeal, we frequently suggest adding some high-gluten flour to help the bread rise better.

WHOLE WHEAT FLOUR

Whole wheat flour is simply flour with the whole wheat berry or kernel milled right in, including the germ and the outer coating of bran, where many of the nutrients are. It comes as all-purpose flour, and I also have seen whole wheat bread flour. Whole wheat flour has to be handled a little differently than all-purpose flour. The whole kernels ground in with the flour inhibit the development of gluten in the bread dough. So if you like plain whole wheat bread, buy some gluten flour to add to it. Many bread machines have a whole wheat setting that gives the dough a little more time, both in the kneading and the rising.

The health benefits of whole wheat bread flour are legion. It has a higher protein content than all-purpose flours, 13 grams per 3½ oz compared to about 10 grams per 3½ oz for all-purpose flour. Many vitamins and minerals present in whole wheat flour are not present in all-purpose flour. We have been inclined to use at least some whole wheat flour in almost all our recipes. Even if you aren't a fan of whole-grain breads, keep 5 pounds or so of a good whole wheat flour around. I like the Robin Hood stone-ground whole wheat.

GLUTEN

Gluten is almost pure protein. It is made by washing the starch from hard wheat flour. When mixed with water, the gluten develops to form a rubbery substance that traps the carbon dioxide made by the yeast. Gluten is especially good when you add fruits, vegetables, or eggs to the dough; these things tend to inhibit or slow the rising power of the yeast. Gluten is also good to add to flours that have a low gluten content, like rye or barley.

OTHER FLOURS AND MEALS

Flours are made from other things besides wheat, like rye, potatoes, rice, and soy beans. Then there are coarser flours called meals: cornmeal, oatmeal, pumpernickel, graham flour, and bran. These should be mixed with high-gluten flour or bread flour, or unbleached all-purpose, to give the yeast some gluten to work with; they help make some marvelous and tasty breads.

Rye flour. You may notice that I call for at least a spoonful of rye flour in a number of recipes, to improve the texture of the bread. Hodgson Mills offers a first-rate whole-grain rye flour. Rye is available as whole rye flour, white rye flour (containing only the starchy endosperm), and the coarser rye meal, also called pumpernickel flour. Rye flour is the best for pumpernickel bread. You may want to try it.

Cornmeal. You will find white or yellow cornmeal. Cornmeal is made from the corn kernels, ground to a sandy texture, coarser than corn flour. You simply have to keep a pound or two of it around. Cornmeal is used in some of my recipes to add to the flavor and texture of bread—for example, Anadama Bread. I roll my English muffins in it. I also usually spread cornmeal on baking sheets, instead of oil or shortening, when I make rolls and breads in the oven. It works perfectly to keep things from sticking and isn't high-fat.

Oatmeal. The kind used for cereal—rolled oats or commercial oatmeal—is also fine to bake with. We use it for breads, of course, but there is nothing like a hot bowl of it on a frosty morning. Then you put what's left in the bread pan.

Graham flour and bran. Graham flour is whole wheat flour in which the starchy endosperm of the wheat kernel is ground fine, but the bran and germ layers are left flaky and coarse. Bran is the outer layer of the grain kernel. A nice touch for whole-grain breads. One of those things best bought in jars.

Potato, rice, and soy flour. Potato flour is made from cooked and dried potatoes, fine ground. Rice flour is made from fine-ground rice kernels. Use the non-waxy kind (not the sweet rice flour, which is used as a thickener). Soy flour is made from fine-milled soy beans. Soybeans are high in protein. Small containers of these various flours are spurs to the imagination.

You should have at least some rye flour around and one or two of the meals, especially the cornmeal and oatmeal, for some delightful and interesting bread. But if you aren't really interested, or can't be bothered, the truth is, for wholesome goodness and nutrition you just can't beat wheat flour—unbleached white or whole wheat—for wonderful-tasting breads and other things.

Water and Other Liquids

Liquids bind all the other ingredients together. Water does it best, and milk is good too, but in an emergency or a fit of inspiration, you can use other things. Those good European loaf recipes like Italian and French use only water. I've tried different kinds of water while seeking the perfect loaf of bread: various brands of spring water, and even melted (white) snow. (I boiled it first.) Unless you live in the vicinity of a toxic dump, most city or well water is going to work pretty much the same as any other water.

Milk will give a denser crumb, more nutrition, and will help preserve the loaf. Most of the books that come with the bread machines, and no small number of supposedly authoritative books, tell you to use dry milk solids. Phooey! Most of of us always have milk (whole-fat, 2%, 1% or skim) in the fridge. Most of the sweet dough recipes in our book suggest milk. We do suggest dry milk in some of the recipes, but if you don't have it around, just use 2 tablespoons of whole milk and complete the liquid measurement called for in the recipe with water; this works just fine.

Fruit juices are called for in some of our recipes. Orange juice, for instance, adds something particularly wonderful. Then there are cranberry juice, apple juice, etc. Most liquids will not bother the yeast; the sweeter liquids, with their natural sugars, will even enhance its working. Flours vary greatly in their ability to absorb liquid, so the amount of liquid given in a recipe is always approximate. You may need to add more or less, but as you gain experience and learn to check the dough ball in the machine after 5 or 10 minutes in the bread machine, you'll know by touching it what to do.

Salt

If you're concerned about salt in your diet, cut it out of something else. Bread is no good without salt. Salt strengthens the gluten and restricts or controls the development of the yeast. It also makes things taste good. I use sea salt. Salt is used on the average of one tsp per 2 cups of flour.

Sugar and Other Sweeteners, Including Honey and Molasses

Yeast feeds on sugar and produces carbon dioxide; this is what helps the bread to rise. Sugar and the other sweeteners sweeten the dough and also act as preservatives. The great French or Italian loaves, which have little or no sugar, are wonderful when fresh, but only last for about a day. Usually within an hour or two that fresh texture and flavor begin to fade. The bread soon becomes stale (of course, then it becomes perfect for French toast).

We often use honey instead of sugar. It tastes a little better and goes to work instantly. We use molasses for Anadama and Dark Rye, and sometimes for Raisin Bread. When using honey and molasses, include them as part of the liquid measurement. Unlike salt, sweeteners aren't necessary. The yeast can feed on the starch in the flour, but the dough will rise more slowly than if a sweetener is added.

Shortening

Shortenings such as lard, butter, margarine, olive oil, vegetable oil, vegetable shortening, and bacon fat make dough easier to work with, which is important when you are using the dough setting on your bread machine, as you will be kneading it for the second rise by hand. Shortening makes for a smoother texture and a somewhat more tender and denser crumb, and adds flavor. It also acts as a preservative. You do not need shortening to make a good loaf of bread, however.

Butter is the one most often suggested, and it does wonderful things for bread, both for flavor and texture. I use lard. Here is why: lard is absorbed by hard wheat flour better than most other shortenings. It leaves virtually no residual flavor, and it is readily available and cheaper than butter. If lard makes you nervous, you can use good old vegetable shortening. If you want to be really creative, and you are planning to make ham sandwiches with the bread, try using rendered bacon fat as shortening.

Oils, especially olive oil, do all the above and add that rich savory flavor that distinguishes our Italian Bread and Pizza Dough. I know of some bakers who insist that for "real" Vienna bread you must use corn oil. Hmm. Bet the Viennese bakers used lard.

With margarine you have to be careful. While it had been generally true that you could substitute margarine for butter in almost everything, times have changed. More and more margarines contain water, whey, and whatever. And while "real" margarine must be 80% fat, things we automatically think of as margarine are now called "spreads," or something like that. The end result is that many brand-name margarines aren't good as shortening anymore—unless you buy a good corn-oil-based margarine.

Other Things You Can Put Into Your Bread Dough

I'm tempted to put "refrigerator gleanings." But in a degree of seriousness, let me suggest a few things that can go into your breads.

EGGS

One of the breads I make most frequently is Challah. The eggs in Challah add a slightly cakelike texture and up the nutritional value a few points. Many roll recipes, especially the sweet rolls, use eggs.

When a recipe calls for an egg, measure it in as part of the liquid. Eggs vary in size, so I frequently say something like: 1 egg + water to fill ⅞ cup. This means: put the egg in the measuring cup, beat it slightly, then add the water to the ⅞ cup level. What size eggs (small, medium, large, etc.) should you use? What about the ratio? The ratio of dry to wet ingredients remains the same. Depending upon how fussy you are, and since the final outcome is not dramatically altered, you can use a small egg in the 1 pound bread machine recipe, a medium egg in the 1½ pound bread machine recipe, and two smalls or an extra-large egg in the 2 pound bread machine recipe. It isn't that crucial, so just use what you have on hand.

Don't leave raw eggs in the bread machine overnight, because the bacteria in raw eggs can grow if they're unrefrigerated.

SPICES

Do not buy brand-name spices. Ridiculously expensive, worthless amounts, and really no better than the inexpensive stuff. Try one of those bulk food or specialty food stores: Indian, Middle Eastern, or Asian. If you buy whole spices and grind them as you need them, you will notice a radical improvement in the quality of what you get. Below are a few essentials.

Cardamom. Depending on where you live, cardamom can be hard to find. I bought a package of whole cardamom from a store specializing in Middle Eastern goodies. The Arabs put cardamom in their coffee. Good idea! I grind my cardamom in my coffee grinder. It has maybe three times the potency of the preground stuff. I call for it in many recipes. You really should get some.

Cinnamon. We buy it buy the pound and use it in many things, not the least of which are Cinnamon Buns, French Spice Loaf, and Raisin Bread.

Nutmeg. Buy whole nutmeg and a grater. We frequently add nutmeg to various sweet doughs for flavor.

Dried chopped onions. Buy a jar of them.

Sesame seeds. Don't make your Italian bread without sesame seeds. Available in health food stores, Asian, Indian, and Middle Eastern grocery stores.

Poppy seeds. Rather necessary for sprinkling on top of braided Challah and various dinner rolls.

POTATO WATER

This is my wife's idea. We eat a lot of potatoes at our house. When she boils potatoes for mashing, she often saves the water, keeping it in a jar in the refrigerator. Then when we go to make a loaf, we use that water in the bread. Potato water not only enhances the flavor of the bread, it also changes the texture. Since potatoes are usually boiled in salted water, you may want to decrease the amount of salt in the recipe if you use potato water.

SOUR MILK

Finding that the milk has soured in our house is almost a cause for rejoicing. Usually Holly grabs it for pancakes, waffles, or her chocolate cake, but it works wonders in the bread machine too. It is fairly difficult to find milk that sours nowadays. You can use buttermilk as a substitute, or a cup of milk with 2 tablespoons of lemon juice or vinegar added. Let it stand for five minutes before you use it.

TOASTED BREAD CRUMBS

Using bread crumbs is an old European trick to get rid of old bread and enhance the flavor of your rye bread. Take ¼ cup of bread crumbs and put them on a cookie sheet under your broiler, if you have one, or in a hot oven if you don't. Toast them until they are brown. Just add them to your regular rye or pumpernickel bread recipe in with the flour measurement.

SOURDOUGH STARTER

You can use a sourdough starter, a sour-sweet, fermenting, starchy batter, in your bread machine. A sourdough starter is also called a sponge. Sourdough, which captures the natural yeast in the air, is what was used by bakers before yeast became readily available. It makes the bread rise by trapping yeast and bacteria in the batter. It is is basically a mixture of flour and liquid, with a little yeast added to get it going, set out to age or sour for several days. It ferments as it ages, developing a nice, sour flavor similar to beer. Milk and sweeteners are added to feed the yeast. Remember the basic proportions of the starter; then follow the instructions for preserving it. Starters usually contain an equal proportion of flour and water. So if you add one cup of starter to your bread machine, you've added approximately ½ cup flour and ½ cup water. Reduce the amount of flour and water in the bread recipe accordingly. If you use sourdough starter in a recipe, you'll only need to add a little extra yeast, less than half the regular amount, to raise the dough.

I have also found that if you have a lively starter, it is best to use the rapid bake cycle if you bake the bread in the bread machine. Better still, make the dough on the dough cycle and bake it in the oven, covered with an egg wash and sesame seeds.

You can buy a good starter at a specialty shop or from a catalogue, or get it from a friend, or you can make your own from the following recipe:

> 1 C unbleached white flour
>
> 1 C warm potato water
>
> 1 tsp sugar or honey
>
> 1 tsp yeast

1. Mix these ingredients together and let them sit in a 1-quart jar covered with a cotton cloth.
2. After a day or so, stir it well and put it in the refrigerator. After another two or three days, it will get nice and sour.
3. When you're ready to bake with it, pour one cup of the starter into the bread machine, along with the ingredients for a basic white, whole wheat, or rye recipe that is reduced by ½ cup flour and ½ cup liquid.

4. Replace what you've taken from the starter jar with the following:

    1 C unbleached white flour

    1 C warm potato water or plain
      warm water, to which you can add ¼ C stale beer

5. Store it in the refrigerator in a clean jar or crock with air space above the mixture. Stir it each day.

Many French bakers make a variation of Sourdough Bread baking without what we think of as a starter; they simply start the bread a day or two before it's baked; see My Own Sourdough Rye Bread (Rob's Rye), which I developed, freely adapting from the French method.

TOOLS

Here are some basic tools you will find handy, in addition to the usual kitchen equipment:

Spray bottle. Buy a small spray bottle for spritzing the dough to help it rise and for spraying the oven to increase the humidity.

Baguette pan. Buy a baguette pan for French bread. You probably won't find one at a yard sale or flea market, but they are worth the cost.

Pulman bread pan. A good investment if you can afford it. If you live in a big city, you may find one at kitchen specialty shop.

Some Easy Recipes
for Getting Started

Let's begin with a brief review: to make bread in your bread machine (or out of it for that matter), you need only these four basic ingredients: flour, water, salt, and yeast. Memorize the following ratio of ingredients (this is for a 1 lb loaf):

2½ C dry to 1 C wet

1 tsp of salt

1 tsp of yeast

The ratio of dry ingredients to wet in a loaf of bread is always approximate. The actual amounts change when you're making a 1½ or 2 or 3 lb loaf, but the proportions remain the same.

Let me add here that most of the recipes in this book are for the 3 common sizes of bread machines, 1 pound, 1½ pound, and 2 pound. If you have a new 3 pound loaf machine, you should be able to double the 1½ lb recipe; but check the dough, you may have to cut back on the water by as much as an ounce. There will be a few recipes which I give only for one size: rolls and some of the specialty and holiday loaves. That's the size I've found works best.

You can prepare any 1½ pound recipe in the 1 pound bread machine on the dough cycle, which means the dough is mixed, kneaded, and has its first rise in the machine, but is baked OUTSIDE the bread machine in the oven. Most 1 lb machine bread pans will not have the room to bake a 1½ lb recipe.

In the same way, you can prepare a 2 pound recipe in a 1½ pound machine on the dough cycle. I'll remind you about this later when we come to the recipes.

For the sake of this quick course, the recipes in this chapter will all be to make a 1 pound loaf. It may be prepared in all 3 sizes of bread machine (1, 1½, or 2 lb) and baked in the machine.

Put the following ingredients into your bread machine, in the order recommended by the manufacturer, regardless of the size of the machine:

2½ C flour   1 C water

1 tsp salt   1 tsp yeast*

*Reminder: all my recipes call for quick or instant, or rapid-rise active dry yeast. If you use regular active dry yeast, add 25% more of it.

When you've loaded your machine, set it on the regular bake cycle, and in a few hours, when the beeper goes off, *Voila!* You will have one great loaf of bread. The above is the good old basic recipe for French bread. In fact, there used to be (maybe there still is) a law in France limiting true French bread to those four ingredients: wheat flour, water, salt and yeast. There was a similar law in 17th-century England. (Of course, the English wouldn't have thought of it as "French" bread.)

Now there is one problem with bread produced by that recipe: it goes stale in a few hours. And, too, people tire of the same old thing, no matter how good it is, and soon they begin fooling around with that basic recipe, adding a bit of this and a bit of that.

It isn't just fooling around, really. Shortening, sugar, and herbs, and various grains and eggs, among other things, add even more flavor to bread, more nutrition, and help preserve it as well. Other things help bread complement the meal, and in some cases even make the bread a meal.

Sugar sweetens it, provides food for the yeast so the bread rises higher, helps the loaves to brown nicely, and makes for a more tender texture. Shortening, which includes oil, butter, vegetable shortening, margarine, and lard, helps the loaf retain moisture, makes the dough easier to work, gives a softer texture, makes a loaf smoother and denser, and of course, adds to the flavor.

Your measuring doesn't have to be that dead-on accurate. Here's why. The moisture content of the flour will vary, the humidity in the air will affect things, the room temperature will vary. So after the machine has kneaded the dough for 5 or 10 minutes, lift the top and look in. Touch the dough ball. If it is wet and sticks to your finger, add a bit more flour, a tablespoon at a time. It should be a bit tacky. Too dry? Add a bit of water, maybe a tablespoon at a time; 99 out of 100 times those additions to the recipes aren't going to affect the bread in any way but to improve it.

Here's another basic recipe:

Basic Bread

2½ C flour	1 C water
1 tsp salt	1 tsp sugar
1 tsp shortening	1 tsp yeast

Put the ingredients in your bread machine and try it on the bake setting. Yield: 1 lb loaf.

Basic American White

2¼ C flour	5 oz water
2 oz milk (whole or whatever)	1 T sugar
1 tsp salt	1 T butter or shortening
1½ tsp yeast	

Load your machine and set it for regular cycle, and start it. Fits in all 3 sizes of bread machine. Yield: 1 lb loaf.

My Challah

Here is a sweet breakfast loaf for Sunday morning. Load your machine and set it for regular cycle, and start it. Or set the timer so it will be done in the morning and nice and warm when you serve it. Fits in all 3 sizes of machine. Yield: 1 lb loaf.

2¼ C all-purpose flour	1 egg plus water to fill ⅞ C
1½ T sugar	1 tsp salt
1 T cooking oil	1½ tsp yeast

FOR CHALLAH GLAZE AND COATING

egg yolk plus 2 tsp water	poppy seeds
2 tsp cinnamon (optional)	½ C raisins (optional)

Aha, you say you like Challah? You can just prepare and bake it in your bread machine on the regular cycle. Or, if you want to try something, make it on the dough cycle and when it comes out, squish it down to a ball. Leave it alone for 5 to 10 minutes; then divide it into three portions and let it rest a few minutes more. Then, roll the three balls of dough into ropes about 14 inches long and braid them loosely. Remember, they are going to double in size, at least, as they rise. Let them rise in a warm place for ¾ hour. Then beat an egg yolk with 2 teaspoons water, and brush it on top of the loaf, sprinkle the poppy seeds on, and bake it in your regular oven for about 35 minutes at 360°F (183°C).

You want a good raisin bread? Add 2 teaspoons of cinnamon and ½ cup raisins, but don't braid the dough; make it into a nice round loaf. Let it rise and bake it in your oven, the same as the Challah.

Sunday Morning Basic White Bread

2¼ C flour	3 oz water
4 oz milk (whole or whatever)	2 T sugar
1 tsp salt	2 T butter
1 tsp cinnamon or cardamom (optional)	1½ tsp yeast

Load your machine and set it for regular cycle, and start it. Fits in all 3 sizes of bread machine. Yield: 1 lb loaf.

About the Recipes

My brother-in law, Ron Kurtz, is one of the smartest people I know and an excellent cook. He is also an engineer, by nature and by education. Ron never makes a loaf of bread without his recipe card in front of him. He has copied all his favorite recipes from various cookbooks, including mine, onto 3 × 5 inch index cards. These he mounts before his very eyes on a specially designed card holder at the special bread machine center in his kitchen. He measures every ingredient into his bread machine. His breads are uniformly excellent.

I am an artist, by nature and training, and tend to be a bit more cavalier in preparing the ingredients for my bread—expecting the muse of bakers to guide my hand. Although my measuring isn't all that precise, my bread is also uniformly excellent, although not uniform. I did force myself to measure carefully, as I prepared the following recipes. And, as I have been told by people whose business it is to know such things, my recipes work.

Before we get into the recipes I want you to note several important things:

1. All the recipes call for regular (preferably unbleached) all-purpose white flour, except, of course, when whole wheat or rye or other specific flours are called for.

2. All the recipes use rapid rise, or instant, active dry yeast. If you are using regular active dry yeast, increase the amount of yeast called for in the recipe by about 25% (¼). Depending on what amount is originally called for in the recipe, increase 1½ teaspoons of instant active dry yeast to 1⅞ teaspoons of regular active dry yeast. Increase 2 teaspoons to 2½ teaspoons. Increase 2½ teaspoons to 3⅛ teaspoons.

3. Use warm water. If it is too cold, warm the water to body temperature before using.

4. The recipes in the Four Basic Breads, Dark Breads, Savory Breads, Fruit Breads, and Miscellaneous Breads sections of this book may all be baked in the bread machine. The recipes in the Oven-Baked Creations section of the book (starting with Oven-Baked Breads) must be baked in the oven, unless noted otherwise.

RECIPES FOR THE BAKE SETTING

This section of the book gives you recipes that you can prepare and bake in the bread machine. In most cases, we have given you recipes for the 3 sizes of bread machine so you can choose the one that fits yours. Recipes for the Bake Setting includes the chapters on Four Basic Breads, Dark Breads, Savory Breads, Fruit Breads, and Miscellaneous Breads.

Four Basic Breads

For most of us, these are the main breads we prepare and bake in the bread machine on the regular setting.

Real Basic Bread

1 lb	1½ lb	2 lb
⅞ C water	1⅛ C water	1½ C water
2¼ C all-purpose flour	3 C all-purpose flour	4 C all-purpose flour
1¼ tsp salt	1½ tsp salt	2 tsp salt
1½ tsp yeast	2 tsp yeast	2½ tsp yeast

Your basic white bread, the most basic of all. For those conscious about diets, fat, cholesterol, whatever, this is the bread. But it doesn't keep well, so if you make it for dinner, eat it with dinner. Prepare and bake it on the regular setting. Follow the instructions for your machine for order of ingredients.

The Other Basic White Bread

This is the other basic white bread. You can vary it, of course, by adding more or less sugar or butter. Or better still, substitute a teaspoon of lard for the butter; it gives an even lighter texture. When you get the recipe just the way you like it, you'll probably memorize it—most of us do. Or you can always write it down on a label and stick it on the side of your machine.

1 lb	1½ lb	2 lb
⅞ C water	1⅛ C water	1½ C water
2¼ C all-purpose flour	3 C all-purpose flour	4 C all-purpose flour
2 tsp sugar	1 T sugar	1½ T sugar
1 tsp lard (butter)	2 tsp lard (butter)	1 T lard (butter)
1¼ tsp salt	1½ tsp salt	1¾ tsp salt
1½ tsp yeast	2 tsp yeast	2½ tsp yeast

Prepare on the rapid or regular cycle. Load the bread pan and follow the operating instructions of your machine.

Whole Wheat Bread

Here is another basic bread. What great toast it makes.

1 lb	1½ lb	2 lb
⅝ C water	⅞ C water	1 C water
¼ C milk	⅓ C milk	½ C milk
1½ C all-purpose flour	2 C all-purpose flour	2½ C all-purpose flour
¾ C whole wheat flour	1 C whole wheat flour	1½ C whole wheat flour
1½ T brown sugar	2 T brown sugar	2½ T brown sugar
1 T butter or lard	1½ T butter	2 T butter or lard
1 tsp salt	1¼ tsp salt	1½ tsp salt
1½ tsp yeast	2 tsp yeast	2½ tsp yeast

Bake on the regular cycle as for the above loaves—or, if your machine has the whole wheat cycle, use it.

Basic Rye Bread

1 lb	1½ lb	2 lb
⅞ C water	1⅛ C water	1½ C water
2 C all-purpose flour	2¼ C all-purpose flour	3 C all-purpose flour
½ C rye flour	¾ C rye flour	1 C rye flour
1½ T brown sugar	2 T brown sugar	2½ T brown sugar
1 T olive oil (or lard)	1½ T olive oil (or lard)	2 T olive oil (or lard)
1¼ tsp salt	1½ tsp salt	2 tsp salt
1 tsp caraway seeds	2 tsp caraway seeds	1 T caraway seeds
1½ tsp yeast	2 tsp yeast	3 tsp yeast

This may be even more basic than the others. Depends on where you're coming from. If your machine has a rye setting, use it. Otherwise use your regular setting.

Now, then, that should take care of the basics. Once you have them down, you can begin improvising. Or try the other recipes, beginning with the dark or whole-grain loaves in the next section.

Dark Breads

Whole Wheat Breads

Whole wheat flour has lots of nutrients in it, but the store-bought whole wheat breads are sometimes dry, fluffy, and boring. Here are some tasty recipes to combat the boring whole wheat syndrome.

Danish No-Nonsense Whole Wheat Bread

1 lb	1½ lb	2 lb
⅞ C milk	1⅛ C milk	1½ C milk
1 T molasses	2 T molasses	3 T molasses
1¾ C whole wheat flour	2 C whole wheat flour	2½ C whole wheat flour
½ C all-purpose flour	1 C all-purpose flour	1½ C all-purpose flour
2 T butter	3 T butter	3½ T butter
1 T brown sugar	1½ T brown sugar	2 T brown sugar
1 tsp salt	1½ tsp salt	2 tsp salt
2 tsp yeast	2½ tsp yeast	3 tsp yeast

Load and bake, on the whole wheat cycle, if your machine has one, the regular cycle if not.

Good Whole Wheat Bread

1 lb	1½ lb	2 lb
1½ C all-purpose flour	2 C all-purpose flour	2½ C all-purpose flour
¾ C whole wheat flour	1 C whole wheat flour	1½ C whole wheat flour
⅝ C water	¾ C water	1 C water
¼ C milk	⅓ C milk	½ C milk
1 T brown sugar.	1½ T brown sugar	2 T brown sugar
1 T butter	1½ T butter	2 T butter
1 tsp salt	1½ tsp salt	2 tsp salt
1½ tsp yeast	2 tsp yeast	2½ tsp yeast

Load and bake, using the whole wheat cycle, if your machine has one, or the regular cycle, if not. It doesn't work well on the rapid cycle.

Honey Whole Wheat Bread

1 lb	1½ lb	2 lb
1¼ C all-purpose flour	2 C all-purpose flour	2½ C all-purpose flour
1 C whole wheat flour	1 C whole wheat flour	1½ C whole wheat flour
1½ T honey	2 T honey	2½ T honey
⅞ C water	1¼ C water	1½ C water
1 T butter	1½ T butter	2 T butter
1 tsp salt	1½ tsp salt	2 (scant) tsp salt
1½ tsp yeast	2 tsp yeast	2½ tsp yeast

Load and bake, using the whole wheat cycle if your machine has one, or the regular cycle, if not. It doesn't work well on the rapid cycle. Here's something my wife suggests for Honey Whole Wheat Bread.

HONEY GLAZE

½ C confectioners' sugar	1½ T milk
¼ C chopped pecans	1 T honey

Mix all the ingredients together and spread the glaze on the bread while the bread is still hot. Serve with scrambled eggs and ham.

Whole Wheat Honey Nut Bread

1 lb	1½ lb	2 lb
1½ C all-purpose flour	2 C all-purpose flour	2½ C all-purpose flour
¾ C whole wheat flour	1 C whole wheat flour	1½ C whole wheat flour
1 egg + water to ⅞ C*	1 egg + water to 1¼ C*	1 egg + water to 1½ C*
1 tsp salt	1½ tsp salt	1½ tsp salt
1½ T honey	2 T honey	2½ T honey
1 T oil	1½ T oil	2 T oil
1½ tsp yeast	2 tsp yeast	2½ tsp yeast
2 T pine nuts or roasted peanuts	2½ T pine nuts or roasted peanuts	3 T pine nuts or roasted peanuts

*See note about eggs in the Ingredients section.

Load and bake as for Good Whole Wheat Bread above, adding the nuts at the beep (if your machine has a fruit beeper), or ten minutes before the end of the kneading. Serve with or without the Honey Glaze as a breakfast loaf.

Athlete's Bread (or Jock's Loaf)

After having endured several seasons of our son's wrestling and the peculiar eating habits of growing high school wrestlers trying to maintain their weight class, we've learned that feeding an athlete requires imagination—and not necessarily steak and eggs every morning. Your kids out for sports or studying dance? This bread alone should do it. Just don't tell them it's healthy or good for them. If you're going to make this, you'll need to get some high-gluten bread flour, or at least some gluten to add to your ingredients.

1 lb	1½ lb	2 lb
1½ C high-gluten flour*	2 C high-gluten flour*	2½ C high-gluten flour*
½ C whole wheat flour	¾ C whole wheat flour	1 C whole wheat flour
¼ C soy flour	¼ C soy flour	⅓ C soy flour
⅞ C water**	1¼ C water**	1½ C water**
2 T dry milk solids**	3 T dry milk solids**	¼ C dry milk solids**
1 T wheat germ	1½ T wheat germ	2 T wheat germ
1½ T honey	2 T honey	2½ T honey
1 tsp salt	1½ tsp salt	1½ tsp salt
1½ tsp yeast	2 tsp yeast	2½ tsp yeast

*Add 1 T to 1½ T gluten and complete the measurement with bread flour if no high-gluten flour is available.
**You can use fruit juice. Or, instead of the liquid and dry milk, you can substitute whole or 2% milk.

Load and bake, using the whole wheat cycle if your machine has it, or the regular cycle if not. This one doesn't work well on the rapid cycle.

Spicy Whole Wheat Bread

This is a bit of delicious madness, especially good with baked ham.

1 lb	1½ lb	2 lb
1¼ C all-purpose flour	2 C all-purpose flour	2½ C all-purpose flour
1 C whole wheat flour	1 C whole wheat flour	1½ C whole wheat flour
1½ T honey	2 T honey	2½ T honey
⅞ C orange juice	1⅛ C orange juice	1½ scant C orange juice
2 tsp grated orange peel	1 T grated orange peel	1½ T grated orange peel
1 T butter	1½ T butter	2 T butter
½ tsp anise seeds	1 scant tsp anise seeds	1¼ tsp anise seeds
1 tsp salt	1½ tsp salt	1½ tsp salt
1½ tsp yeast	2 tsp yeast	2½ tsp yeast

Bake the same as for Whole Wheat Honey Nut Bread, omitting the glaze. Think about serving it with cream cheese and apricot preserves. And if you want to be a little Lithuanian (those people know how to eat), add a little horseradish to the apricot preserves. Sounds nutty, I know, but it is delightful.

Ryes

Even if your bread machine doesn't have a rye setting, you'll find it does a good job at making rye bread, especially if you use the whole wheat setting. Rye flour doesn't have much gluten, so it doesn't rise like other flours. This is why there is a bit more yeast and extra white flour in the recipes. You can adjust the recipes to your own taste, particularly in the amount of fennel and/or caraway seeds, and the proportion of rye flour you use.

Mormon Rye Bread

1 lb	1½ lb	2 lb
2 C all-purpose flour	2½ C all-purpose flour	3 C all-purpose flour
½ C rye flour	¾ C rye flour	1 C rye flour
1 T dark brown sugar	1½ T dark brown sugar	2 T dark brown sugar
1 T dry milk	1½ T dry milk	2 T dry milk
¾ C water	1⅛ C water	1⅓ C water
1 small egg*	1 medium egg*	1 extra-large egg*
1 T cooking oil	1½ T cooking oil	2 T cooking oil
1 tsp salt	1½ tsp salt	1½ tsp salt
1½ tsp yeast	2 tsp yeast	2½ tsp yeast
1 tsp caraway seeds*	2 tsp caraway seeds*	1 T caraway seeds*

*See note about eggs in the Ingredients section. Use fennel instead of caraway seeds if you wish.

Load and bake on the rye or whole wheat setting according to your machine's instructions.

Swedish Rye Bread

1 lb	1½ lb	2 lb
1¾ C all-purpose flour	2¼ C all-purpose flour	2¾ C all-purpose flour
½ C rye flour	¾ C rye flour	1¼ C rye flour
1 C water	1¼ C water	1½ C water
2 T brown sugar	2½ T brown sugar	3 T brown sugar
1 T cocoa	1½ T cocoa	2 T cocoa
1 tsp salt	1½ tsp salt	1½ tsp salt
½ tsp grated orange rind	1 tsp grated orange rind	1½ tsp grated orange rind
1 T lard	1 T +1 tsp lard	1½ T lard
½ tsp fennel seeds	1 tsp fennel seeds	1½ tsp fennel seeds
1½ tsp yeast	2 tsp yeast	2½ tsp yeast

Load and bake on the rye or whole wheat setting according to your machine's instructions. Now, that's the rye you put your corned beef on.

Dark Rye Bread

Here are those toasted bread crumbs I mentioned in the Ingredients section. You'll find this loaf doesn't rise too high.

1 lb	1½ lb	2 lb
1¼ C all-purpose flour	1¾ C all-purpose flour	2 C all-purpose flour
½ C whole wheat flour	¾ C whole wheat flour	1 C whole wheat flour
½ C rye flour	¾ C rye flour	1 C rye flour
⅞ C of water	1¼ C of water	1½ C of water
1 T cocoa	1½ T cocoa	2 T cocoa
1 T molasses	1½ T molasses	2 T molasses
2 tsp caraway seeds	1 T caraway seeds	1 T caraway seeds
¼ tsp ground ginger	½ tsp ground ginger	½ tsp ground ginger
1 T lard	1½ T lard	2 T lard
1 tsp salt	1 tsp salt	1½ tsp salt
1¾ tsp yeast	2 tsp yeast	2¼ tsp yeast
¼ C toasted bread crumbs*	⅓ C toasted bread crumbs*	½ C toasted bread crumbs*

* See the Ingredients section, in case you've forgotten how to make these.

Load and bake on the rye or whole wheat setting according to your machine's instructions.

Pumpernickel Bread

By adding the coffee and coarse-ground cornmeal to the Dark Rye Bread recipe, we have pumpernickel—the acceptable platform for Reuben sandwiches, or just loading with ham, Swiss cheese, pickles, lettuce, tomato, and serving with a good dark beer.

1 lb	1½ lb	2 lb
1 C all-purpose flour	1½ C all-purpose flour	2 C all-purpose flour
½ C whole wheat flour	¾ C whole wheat flour	1 C whole wheat flour
¾ C coarse rye flour	¾ C coarse rye flour	1 C coarse rye flour
¼ C cornmeal	⅓ C cornmeal	½ C cornmeal
1½ T cocoa	2 T cocoa	2½ T cocoa
⅞ C strong coffee	1⅛ C coffee	1½ C coffee
1½ T molasses	2 T	2½ T molasses
2 tsp lard	1 T lard	1½ T lard
1 T caraway seeds	1½ T caraway seeds	1½ T caraway seeds
1 tsp salt	1½ tsp salt	1½ tsp salt
2 tsp yeast	2¼ tsp yeast	2½ tsp yeast

It's one of those hefty loaves with lots of opposition to the yeast. Bake it on the whole wheat or rye cycle. Even better, prepare it on the dough cycle, knead it for a few minutes by hand, let it rise, and bake as a conventional round loaf in your oven. That leads us to the reason for pumpernickel bread—the Reuben Sandwich.

THE REUBEN SANDWICH

Make dark bread slices, spread with Russian dressing, pile up with corned beef, then add some Swiss or Gruyere cheese and a nice glob of sauerkraut. Grill the sandwich in a mixture of butter and olive oil in an iron pan or griddle. Serve with thick-cut French fries, cole slaw, and dark beer.

Onion Rye Bread

Actually a pretty fair Reuben, or Rachel, sandwich can be made with the following bread. Furthermore, it shows that those little jars of dried onions can serve a useful purpose. Depending on how much energy or time you have, you can sauté fresh onions in butter and then add them instead of the dried onions. It's your bread.

1 lb	1½ lb	2 lb
1¼ C all-purpose flour	1¾ C all-purpose flour	2 C all-purpose flour
¾ C rye flour	1 C rye flour	1¼ C rye flour
¼ C whole wheat flour	½ C whole wheat flour	¾ C whole wheat flour
1 T brown sugar	1½ T brown sugar	2 T brown sugar
⅞ C water	1⅛ C water	1⅓ C water
1 small egg*	1 medium egg*	1 extra-large egg*
1 T dried onions**	2 T dried onions**	3 T dried onions**
1 tsp salt	1½ tsp salt	1½ tsp salt
1 tsp caraway seeds	1½ tsp caraway seeds	1 T caraway seeds
1½ T lard	2 T lard	2½ T lard
½ tsp black pepper	¾ tsp black pepper	1 tsp black pepper
1½ tsp yeast	2 tsp yeast	2½ tsp yeast

*See note about eggs in the Ingredients section.
**If you use fresh onions, use ½ of a medium-sized onion for the 1 or 1½ lb bread machine and ¾ of a medium-sized onion for the 2 lb bread machine.

It's a rye. Bake as such, or on the whole wheat setting, if you don't have a rye setting.

Whole-Grain Breads

This section is for the health enthusiasts among us, in reaction to the terrible bread available before the bread machine.

Cracked Wheat Bread

1 lb	1½ lb	2 lb
1½ C all-purpose flour	2 C all-purpose flour	2½ C all-purpose flour
½ C whole wheat flour	¾ C whole wheat flour	1 C whole wheat flour
¼ C cracked wheat*	⅓ C cracked wheat*	½ C cracked wheat*
⅞ C water	1¼ C water	1½ C water
1 T honey	1½ T honey	2 T honey
1 T butter	1½ T butter	2 T butter
1 tsp salt	1½ tsp salt	1½ tsp salt
1½ tsp yeast	2 tsp yeast	2½ tsp yeast

*If you can't find cracked wheat, substitute wheat germ in its place.

Prepare and bake on the whole-wheat or regular cycle.

Multi-Grain Bread

If you positively had to live on bread alone, this one just might do it.

1 lb	1½ lb	2 lb
1½ C bread flour	2 C bread flour	2½ C bread flour
¼ C oats	½ C oats	¾ C oats
¼ C wheat flour	½ C whole wheat flour	¾ C whole wheat flour
½ C water	⅝ C water	¾ C water
½ C milk	¾ C milk	1 C milk
2 T bran / bran flakes	2½ T bran / bran flakes	3 T bran / bran flakes
1 T honey	1½ T honey	2 T honey
2 T wheat germ	2½ T wheat germ	3 T wheat germ
1 tsp salt	1½ tsp salt	2 tsp salt
1 T butter	1½ T butter	2 T butter
2 tsp yeast	2¼ tsp yeast	2½ tsp yeast

Load and bake on the regular setting.

Anadama Bread

That story about the Yankee sea captain who married a woman who couldn't make bread may or may not be true. Would a captain do the unthinkable and curse his wife, saying "Anna, damn her"? Is it possible that this recipe, which he is alleged to have given her, came from still another wife, in yet another port?

1 lb	1½ lb	2 lb
1½ C all-purpose flour	2¼ C all-purpose flour	3 C all-purpose flour
½ C cornmeal	⅔ C cornmeal	¾ C cornmeal
¼ C whole wheat flour	½ C whole wheat flour	¾ C whole wheat flour
⅝ C water	⅞ C water	1⅛ C water
¼ C milk	⅓ C milk	½ C milk
1 T molasses*	1 T + 1 tsp molasses*	2 T molasses*
1 T oil	1½ T oil	2 T oil
1 tsp salt	1½ tsp salt	1½ tsp salt
1½ tsp yeast	2 tsp yeast	2½ tsp yeast

*You can use brown sugar instead of molasses.

Load and bake on the regular cycle.

Fruity Bran Bread

1 lb	1½ lb	2 lb
2 C all-purpose flour	2½ C all-purpose flour	3 C all-purpose flour
½ C bran*	¾ C bran*	1 C bran*
⅜ C water	½ C water	¾ C water
½ C milk	¾ C milk	¾ C milk
1 tsp salt	1½ tsp salt	1½ tsp salt
1½ T brown sugar	2 T brown sugar	2½ T brown sugar
1 T butter	1½ T butter	2 T butter
¼ C raisins	⅓ C raisins	½ C raisins
¼ C walnuts or pecans	⅓C walnuts or pecans	½ C walnuts or pecans
1 T chopped dates	1½ T chopped dates	2 T chopped dates
1½ tsp yeast	2 tsp yeast	2½ tsp yeast

*You can use crushed bran flakes instead of bran.

A high-fiber tasty loaf of bread. Load and bake on the regular setting.

Savory Breads

The smell of baking savory breads is breathtaking. It produces the most mouth-watering air freshener you could want, permeating your home with a delicious natural fragrance that drives men wild (kind of makes you think twice about the herbs you pick). The breads, eaten as snacks, platforms for other goodies, or served with a meal, add depth and enhance, if not improve, the flavor of your favorite stews and soups. These loaves are best in summer with herbs fresh from your garden. Only your imagination can limit what you can do with combinations. But here are a few basic recipes to get you started.

Herb Breads

Dill Bread

1 lb	1½ lb	2 lb
⅜ C water	⅝ C water	⅞ C water
½ C plain yogurt	¾ C plain yogurt	1 C plain yogurt
1 small egg*	1 medium egg*	1 extra-large egg*
2¼ C all-purpose flour	3 C all-purpose flour	4 C all-purpose flour
1 tsp salt	1½ tsp salt	2 tsp salt
1 T butter	1½ T butter	2 T butter
1 T fresh dill, chopped	1½ T fresh dill, chopped	2 T fresh dill, chopped
1½ tsp yeast	2 tsp yeast	2½ tsp yeast

*See note about eggs in the Ingredients section.

Load and bake according to your machine's instructions on the regular setting. Great plain or served with Blue Cheese Spread.

BLUE CHEESE SPREAD

¼ pound blue cheese	¼ pound butter
½ C minced black olives	¼ C wine vinegar
4 slices crisply fried bacon, crumbled	

For spreading on the Dill Bread and Herb Bread, try this. By the way, cheap domestic blue cheese is good enough. Soften the butter and cheese; then combine all the ingredients, adding the bacon last of all.

Herb Bread

1 lb	1½ lb	2 lb
2¼ C bread flour	3 C bread flour	4 C bread flour
⅞ C water	1¼ C water	1½ C water
1 T sugar	1½ T sugar	2 T sugar
1 tsp salt	1½ tsp salt	2 tsp salt
1 T butter	1½ T butter	2 T butter
2 tsp fresh minced parsley	1 T fresh minced parsley	1½ T fresh minced parsley
½ tsp savory*	1 tsp savory*	1½ tsp savory*
½ tsp thyme or sage*	1 tsp thyme or sage*	1½ tsp thyme or sage*
½ tsp marjoram*	1 tsp marjoram*	1½ tsp marjoram*
1½ tsp yeast	2 tsp yeast	2½ tsp yeast

*Use fresh herbs if possible, but increase to a full teaspoon of each herb.

Load and bake according to your machine's instructions on the regular or the rapid-rise setting. Prepare the same as for Dill Bread. Use your Blue Cheese Spread on this bread also.

PARSLEY BUTTER

2 tsp fresh chives, minced	¼ pound butter, softened
¼ C minced fresh parsley	1 tsp lemon juice
1 clove of garlic, pressed or crushed	

Combine the softened butter with the rest of the ingredients. Sure looks like the innards of Chicken Kiev to me.

Herb Bread Two

1 lb	1½ lb	2 lb
2¼ C all-purpose flour	3 C all-purpose flour	4 C all-purpose flour
1 small egg + water to fill ⅞ cup*	1 medium egg + water to fill 1¼ cup*	1 large egg + water to fill 1½ cup*
juice of ¼ lemon	juice of ½ lemon	juice of ¾ lemon
1½ T sugar	2 T sugar	2½ T sugar
1 tsp salt	1½ tsp salt	2 tsp salt
1 T butter	1½ T butter	2 T butter
½ tsp celery seeds	1 tsp celery seeds	1½ tsp celery seeds
½ tsp dried sage	1 tsp dried sage	1½ tsp dried sage
1 T dried onions	1 T + 1 tsp dried onions	1 T + 2 tsp dried onions
1 T dry milk	1½ T dry milk	2 T dry milk
1½ tsp yeast	2 tsp yeast	2½ tsp yeast

*See note about eggs in the Ingredients section.

Load and bake according to your machine's instructions on the rapid or regular setting. Serve plain or with Blue Cheese Spread or Parsley Butter, or use it for an open-faced cheese sandwich by toasting the slices, laying the cheese on it, and melting it in whatever you use for such things.

Cheese Breads

Cheese is as good in bread as on it. From mild old American cheese to sharp Cheddar or blues, bread goes from simply enhancing a meal to becoming one when cheese is added to the ingredients. The simplest cheese bread can be done almost as an afterthought: throw a tablespoon or two of Parmesan or Romano cheese in with your basic bread. If you're watching your diet, use cheese and leave out the other shortening. Try the following recipes, or make your own variations by using different cheeses.

Three-Cheese Bread

1 lb	1½ lb	2 lb
2¼ C all-purpose flour	3 C all-purpose flour	4 C all-purpose flour
⅞ C water	1¼ C water	1½ C water
1 T vegetable oil*	1½ T vegetable oil*	2 T vegetable oil*
2 T blue cheese	2½ T blue cheese	3 T blue cheese
1 T grated Parmesan	1½ T grated Parmesan	2 T grated Parmesan
½ C shredded cheddar	¾ C shredded cheddar	1 C shredded cheddar
1 tsp sugar	2 tsp sugar	1 T sugar
1 tsp salt	1½ tsp salt	2 tsp salt
½ tsp dry mustard	¾ tsp dry mustard	1 tsp dry mustard
½ tsp black pepper	¾ tsp black pepper	1 tsp black pepper
1½ tsp yeast	2 tsp yeast	2½ tsp yeast

*You could use olive oil instead.

Load and bake on the rapid or regular setting.

Cheese and Pepper Loaf*

1 lb	1½ lb	2 lb
2¼ C all-purpose flour	3 C all-purpose flour	4 C all-purpose flour
⅞ C water	1¼ C water	1½ C water
1 T olive oil	1½ T olive oil	2 T olive oil
1 T sugar	1½ T sugar	2 T sugar
1 tsp salt	1½ tsp salt	2 tsp salt
½ tsp thyme	1 tsp thyme	1½ tsp thyme
1 tsp ground black pepper	1½ tsp ground black pepper	2 tsp ground black pepper
½ C grated sharp cheddar cheese	¾ C grated sharp cheddar cheese	1 C grated sharp cheddar cheese
1½ tsp yeast	2 tsp yeast	2½ tsp yeast

*Optional additions for added zest (all 3 sizes): 1 T Worcestershire sauce, ½ tsp dry mustard, ¼ tsp cayenne pepper

Load and bake according to your machine's instructions on the rapid or regular setting. If you have bits and pieces of ham or bologna, summer sausage, or various kinds of dry cheese, mince them and toss them in the pan, too.

Cheese and Pepperoni Bread

If you have some pepperoni in the fridge, and you really should, then you have the makings for this delicious bread.

1 lb	1½ lb	2 lb
2¼ C all-purpose flour	3 C all-purpose flour	4 C all-purpose flour
⅞ C water	1¼ C water	1½ C water
1 T olive oil	1½ T olive oil	2 T olive oil
1 T sugar	1½ T sugar	2 T sugar
1 tsp salt	1½ tsp salt	2 tsp salt
½ tsp dried thyme	1 tsp dried thyme	1½ tsp dried thyme
1 tsp ground black pepper	1½ tsp ground black pepper	2 tsp ground black pepper
½ tsp dried oregano*	¾ tsp dried oregano*	1 tsp dried oregano*
¼ tsp garlic powder*	½ tsp garlic powder*	¾ tsp garlic powder*
½ tsp onion powder*	¾ tsp onion powder*	1 tsp onion powder*
½ C pepperoni, diced	⅔ C pepperoni, diced	¾ C pepperoni, diced
¼ C grated cheddar	⅓ C grated cheddar	½ C grated cheddar
2 T grated Parmesan	2½ T grated Parmesan	3 T grated Parmesan
1½ tsp yeast	2 tsp yeast	2½ tsp yeast

*If you want to, you can substitute Italian seasoning for the oregano, garlic, and onion powder: 1 T for the l lb; 1½ T for the 1½ lb machine, and 2 T for the 2 lb machine.

If you have the time or inclination, first heat the olive oil in a frying pan, add a clove or two (or three) of fresh garlic and maybe half an onion, chopped, and sauté them for a few minutes. Throw the oregano and pepperoni into the frying pan, and sauté for a minute. Then add all of it to the bread pan. Bake on the regular setting.

Vegetable Breads

Spinach-Zucchini Bread

I'll start with this because it is another way to use up zucchini, which you'll need if you have a couple of zucchini plants in your garden. Zucchini are the rabbits of the vegetable kingdom.

1 lb	1½ lb	2 lb
2¼ C all-purpose flour	3 C all-purpose flour	4 C all-purpose flour
1 small egg + water to fill ⅝ C*	1 medium egg + water to fill 1 C*	1 extra-large egg + water to fill 1¼ C*
½ C grated, peeled zucchini	¾ C grated, peeled zucchini	1 C grated, peeled zucchini
1 T butter	1½ T butter	2 T butter
½ C spinach**	¾ cup spinach**	1 cup spinach**
1 tsp salt	1½ tsp salt	2 tsp salt
1½ tsp yeast	2 tsp yeast	2½ tsp yeast

*See note about eggs in the Ingredients section.
**Use frozen chopped spinach that has been thawed, drained, and pressed almost dry in a colander.

Load and bake according to your machine's instructions on the regular setting.

Onion Bread

1 lb	1½ lb	2 lb
2¼ C all-purpose flour	3 C all-purpose flour	4 C all-purpose flour
¾ C water	1⅛ C water	1¼ C water
1 T olive oil	1¼ T olive oil	1½ T olive oil
1 T butter	1½ T butter	2 T butter
½ C chopped onions	¾ C chopped onions	1 C chopped onions
1 T sugar	1 T + 1 tsp sugar	1½ T sugar
1 tsp salt	1¼ tsp salt	1½ tsp salt
½ tsp celery salt	¾ tsp celery salt	1 tsp celery salt
1½ tsp yeast	2 tsp yeast	2½ tsp yeast

Melt the butter with the olive oil and sauté the onions. Then add to the water; this cools everything down nicely. Add remaining ingredients and bake on the regular or fast setting.

Tomato Bread

I wanted to see if I could come up with a nice red bread to use with the Spinach-Zucchini Bread for tricolor bread slices, for an Italian motif. This is what I came up with. Then my brilliant daughter Kirsten refined it for me.

1 lb	1½ lb	2 lb
2¼ C all-purpose flour	3 C all-purpose flour	4 C all-purpose flour
⅞ C water	1¼ C water	1½ C water
1 T olive oil	1½ T olive oil	2 T olive oil
1 T tomato paste	1½ T tomato paste	2 T tomato paste
1 T sugar	1½ T sugar	2 T sugar
1 tsp salt	1½ tsp salt	2 tsp salt
¼ tsp pepper	½ tsp pepper	¾ tsp pepper
1 tsp dry basil*	1½ tsp dry basil*	2 tsp dry basil*
1½ tsp yeast	2 tsp yeast	2½ tsp yeast

*You might want to add lots of *fresh* basil, oregano, chives, and, of course, garlic and parsley. You can prepare them as for the Cheese and Pepperoni Bread, sautéing the onion, garlic, and herbs in the olive oil before adding them to the bread machine.

Combine the tomato paste, olive oil, and water (and the herbs if you use them) before adding them to the bread pan. Load and bake according to your machine's instructions on the rapid or regular setting.

This bread serves as a perfect platform, as one of my kids put it, on which to melt some mozzarella, or provolone, and serve it as a little light luncheon treat—along with a nice husky dry California red wine, or even a Chianti.

Carrot Bread

Think of it as a savory carrot cake.

1 lb	1½ lb	2 lb
2 C all-purpose flour	2½ C all-purpose flour	3¼ C all-purpose flour
¼ C whole wheat flour	½ C whole wheat flour	¾ C whole wheat flour
⅞ C water	1¼ C water	1½ C water
½ C shredded carrots	¾ C shredded carrots	1 C shredded carrots
1½ T brown sugar	2 T brown sugar	2½ T brown sugar
1 tsp salt	1½ tsp salt	2 tsp salt
1 T butter	1½ T butter	2 T butter
¼ C walnuts*	⅓ C walnuts*	½ C walnuts*
1 tsp cinnamon	1¼ tsp cinnamon	1½ tsp cinnamon
1½ tsp yeast	2 tsp yeast	2½ tsp yeast

*Optional.

Load and bake according to your machine's instructions on the regular setting. Serve plain or with Cinnamon Butter. (Cinnamon Butter, you ask?)

CINNAMON BUTTER

¼ lb softened butter   1 tsp or more cinnamon

2 T sifted confectioners' sugar

Cream the ingredients together. Spread on bread as desired.

Fruit Breads

While it probably goes without saying that the most popular fruit bread is raisin bread, there are others. In fact there are as many varieties of fruit breads as there are fruits. Offhand, I can't think of a single fruit that doesn't lend itself to a good loaf of bread (Kiwi did someone say? Okay, then, how about grapefruit?) Maybe kumquats would work. Anyway, here are just a few recipes to get you started.

Raisin Breads

Is there anything that starts the juices running in the morning more quickly than the smell of raisin bread toasting? (I mean besides that.) When we first got our bread machine, my wife baked raisin bread almost every day. The first recipe is easy and it always works. (But if you really like raisin bread and are willing to go to extra lengths to get the best raisin bread you've ever eaten, try one of my Rolled Raisin Breakfast loaves in the Dough Setting section of the book.)

PLUMPING RAISINS

To begin, if your raisins are a little dry (or even if they aren't), you can plump them up by soaking them in hot water for 15 minutes. So, before you do anything else, measure the amount of water you are going to need. You'll use that water in the bread. With that in mind, you may want to try this: put the water in a microwave-safe bowl and add a jigger of brandy or dark rum to the water. Now measure the correct amount of raisins and put them in the liquid. Put the bowl into the microwave and heat them for about 1½ minutes on high. Or you can just pour the boiling liquid over the raisins. After a few minutes, drain the raisins and let the liquid cool. Put the drained raisins in a small bowl with one tablespoon of flour and toss them a moment to coat them with flour. You will use both the liquid and the raisins in the recipe.

Many, if not most, of the newer machines beep to let you know when to add fruit and nuts to the dough. Some also have a special kneader blade for raisin bread. If your machine has neither, try checking the kneading times on your machine. Add the raisins after much of the kneading has been done, about 15 minutes after you've started the bread.

Real Raisin Bread

1 lb	1½ lb	2 lb
2¼ C all-purpose flour	3 C all-purpose flour	4 C all-purpose flour
⅞ C liquid*	1⅛ C liquid*	1½ C liquid*
1½ T brown sugar	2 T brown sugar	2½ T brown sugar
1 tsp salt	1½ tsp salt	2 tsp salt
1½ T butter	2 T butter	2½ T butter
1 tsp cinnamon	1½ tsp cinnamon	2 tsp cinnamon
⅓ C raisins, plumped	½ C raisins, plumped	¾ C raisins, plumped
2 tsp yeast	2½ tsp yeast	3 tsp yeast

*This is the water in which you soaked the raisins. Include the liquor in your liquid measurements. See instructions for plumping raisins, above.

1. Load and bake the ingredients according to your machine's instructions on the regular setting.
2. When done, remove the loaf from the pan immediately and place on a rack. While still warm, glaze with the Orange Glaze or the Vanilla Glaze described below.

What follows is really my wife's doing. For her, raisin bread isn't raisin bread unless there is some substance glistening on top.

VANILLA GLAZE

2 drops of vanilla	2 tsp milk
½ C confectioners' sugar	1 pinch of salt
¼ C finely chopped walnuts or pecans	

Combine the vanilla and milk and stir into the salt and sugar until the sugar is fully dissolved. When it is at spreading consistency, add the walnuts or pecans.

ORANGE GLAZE

¾ C confectioners' sugar	2 tsp soft butter
1 T orange-flavored liqueur*	¼ C finely chopped walnuts or pecans

*In its absence, use orange juice.

Cream together the butter and sugar and add the liqueur or orange juice. When it is at spreading consistency, add the walnuts or pecans.

Apple–Raisin Bread

1 lb	1½ lb	2 lb
2¼ C all-purpose flour	3 C all-purpose flour	4 C all-purpose flour
1½ T brown sugar	2 T brown sugar	2½ T brown sugar
1 tsp salt	1½ tsp salt	2 tsp salt
¾ C water	1 C water	1¼ C water
2 T butter	2½ T butter	3 T butter
1 tsp cinnamon	1½ tsp cinnamon	2 tsp cinnamon
⅓ C peeled chopped apples	½ C peeled, chopped apples	¾ C peeled chopped apples
¼ C raisins	⅓ C raisins	½ C raisins
1½ tsp yeast	2 tsp yeast	2½ tsp yeast

1. Sauté the apples in the butter in a frying pan. When they are fairly soft, add the cinnamon and sugar. Put the apples in a bowl and add the raisins; cool. Put all the other ingredients in the bread machine. Add the apples and raisins at the fruit beeper or 5 minutes before the end of the kneading.
2. Bake the bread according to the machine's directions on the regular setting. Some there are who say: when done, and while still warm, spread with a glaze (see glazes on previous page).

Other Fruit Breads

Cranberry Bread

1 lb	1½ lb	2 lb
2¼ C all-purpose flour	3 C all-purpose flour	4 C all-purpose flour
1½ T sugar	2 T sugar	2½ T sugar
⅞ C cranberry juice	1¼ C cranberry juice	1½ C cranberry juice
1 tsp salt	1½ tsp salt	2 tsp salt
2 T cranberry sauce or ¼ C fresh berries	3 T cranberry sauce or ⅓ C fresh berries	4 T cranberry sauce or ½ C fresh berries
1 T butter	1½ T butter	2 T butter
1½ T yeast	2 T yeast	2½ T yeast

Load and bake according to your machine's instructions on the rapid or regular setting.

Apricot Bread

1 lb	1½ lb	2 lb
2 C all-purpose flour	2¾ C all-purpose flour	3¼ C all-purpose flour
¼ C whole wheat four	½ C whole wheat flour	¾ C whole wheat flour
1 T sugar	1½ T sugar	2 T sugar
1 tsp salt	1½ tsp salt	2 tsp salt
1 T butter	1½ T butter	2 T butter
1 small egg + apricot nectar to fill ⅞ C	1 medium egg + apricot nectar to fill 1¼ C	1 extra-large egg + apricot nectar to fill 1½ C
juice of ¼ lemon	juice of ½ + lemon	juice of ¾ + lemon
1 T apricot preserves or ¼ C chopped dried apricots	2 T apricot preserves or ⅓ C chopped dried apricots	3 T apricot preserves or ½ C chopped dried apricots
1½ tsp yeast	2 tsp yeast	2½ tsp yeast

Load and bake on the regular bake setting according to the instructions of your machine. When done, remove from the pan and place on a rack to cool. Serve plain or top with Quick and Easy Apricot Glaze or Apricot Butter.

QUICK AND EASY APRICOT GLAZE

Spread ¼ C apricot preserves onto the Apricot Bread.

You can make the Apricot Butter below to go with your Apricot Bread, or with another bread.

APRICOT BUTTER

2 T apricot preserves	4 oz butter
1 or 2 T confectioners' sugar	1 T apricot liqueur (optional)

Mix well together. Spread on bread.

Banana Bread

When bananas are very ripe—really dark—they are sweet and perfect for cooking, and usually on sale. Buy them and try the following: this too is a wonderful breakfast loaf.

1 lb	1½ lb	2 lb
1 very ripe banana	1 very ripe banana	1 very ripe large banana
1 small egg*	1 medium egg*	*1 extra-large egg*
water*	water*	water*
1 T banana liqueur or rum	1 T banana liqueur or rum	1 T banana liqueur or rum
2¼ C all-purpose flour	3 C all-purpose flour	4 C all-purpose flour
2 T butter	2½ T butter	3 T butter
1 T sugar	1½ T sugar	2 T sugar
1 tsp salt	1½ tsp salt	2 tsp salt
1 tsp cinnamon	1¼ tsp cinnamon	1½ tsp cinnamon
1½ tsp yeast	2 tsp yeast	2½ tsp yeast

*See note about eggs in Ingredients section. See Step 1 for amount of water.

1. Put the mushy banana in a measuring cup and beat it up. Add the egg and mix the two. Add the water and the banana liqueur or rum, if you have some, to bring the total liquid to 1 cup for the 1 lb loaf, 1¼ cups for the 1½ lb loaf, and 1½ cups for the 2 lb loaf.
2. Load the other ingredients and bake according to your machine's instructions on the regular setting.
3. When done, remove the loaf from the pan immediately and place on a rack to cool. You can coat the top with Orange Glaze or Vanilla Frosting, if you want. Serve it warm with dark coffee, preferably espresso.

Orangiest Orange Bread

Now this is the *pièce de résistance*—my own invention and one of the finest loaves of bread ever. *The* orange bread, the breakfast loaf without peer. Perfect when Valencia oranges are available. If you don't have Grand Marnier in your cabinet, try some cheap orange liqueur. We have found that in cooking, the cheaper, industrial-strength brandies and liqueurs impart more of their flavor than the better or more expensive brands, which by their very nature are more refined and delicate. This is also one of the prettiest loaves you will have seen. I'm also including only two recipes, regular and medium. You can make the medium loaf in the 1½ or 2 lb bread machine.

Regular (1, 1½ lb, or 2 lb)	Medium (1½ or 2 lb)
2¼ C all-purpose flour	3 C all-purpose flour
¾ (scant) C orange juice	1 C orange juice
1 T orange liqueur	1 T orange liqueur
1 heaping T marmalade	2 T marmalade
1½ T brown sugar	2 T brown sugar
1 tsp salt	1½ tsp salt
2 T butter	3 T butter
1 T orange zest (save ½ tsp)*	1½ T orange zest (save ½ T)*
1½ tsp yeast	2 tsp yeast
¼ C raisins**	¼ C raisins**
¼ T cinnamon**	¼ T cinnamon**
¼ T ground cloves**	¼ T ground cloves**

*The reserved orange zest is used in the Orange Butter, below.
**Optional.

Load and bake according to your machine's instructions on the regular setting. Lock the kitchen door. Remove the loaf from the pan onto a rack to cool. While it's cooling, make the Orange Butter.

ORANGE BUTTER

1 stick (4 oz) of softened butter	1 T orange liqueur
1 heaping T confectioners' sugar	1 T marmalade
½ T orange zest	

Mix well and put the Orange Butter in a small serving dish.

Nut Breads

Nuts in bread not only improve the taste, they make the crust crunchy and increase the amount of protein in the bread. Here are a few recipes, but if you have spare nuts around the house, don't be afraid to add them to your favorite bread recipe. Remember, nuts and fruits tend to inhibit the rising of the bread, so you may prefer to use bread flour or add some gluten flour to the all-purpose flour.

Date-Nut Bread

Not exactly the great stuff that comes out of cans, but pretty good anyway. If you like the other, you'll like this.

1 lb	1½ lb	2 lb
1¾ C flour	2¼ C flour	2¾ C flour
½ C whole wheat flour	¾ C whole wheat flour	1¼ C whole wheat flour
¾ C water	1 C water	1 C water
⅛ C milk	¼ C milk	½ C milk
1½ T brown sugar	2 T brown sugar	2½ T brown sugar
1 tsp salt	1½ tsp salt	2 tsp salt
2 T butter	2½ T butter	3 T butter
¼ C walnuts or pecans, chopped	⅓ C walnuts or pecans, chopped	½ C walnuts or pecans, chopped
¼ C dates, chopped	⅓ C dates, chopped	½ C dates, chopped
2 tsp yeast	2½ tsp yeast	3 tsp yeast

1. Load and bake on the regular setting according to the instructions of your bread machine.
2. Serve plain, or while still warm, cover it with one of the Raisin Bread glazes (see page 47).

Pistachio Bread

Try this if someone gives you a load of pistachios, as they did to us once.

1 lb	1½ lb	2 lb
2¼ C all-purpose flour	3 C all-purpose flour	4 C all-purpose flour
⅞ C water	1¼ C water	1½ C water
2 T honey	2½ T honey	3 T honey
1 tsp salt	1½ tsp salt	2 tsp salt
1 T butter	1½ T butter	2 T butter
½ C shelled pistachios	¾ C shelled pistachios	1 C shelled pistachios
1½ tsp yeast	2 tsp yeast	2½ tsp yeast

1. Load and bake on the regular setting according to the instructions of your bread machine.
2. Serve plain, or while still warm, cover it with one of the Raisin Bread glazes (see page 47).

Walnut Bread

Try this if you have a load of walnuts.

1 lb	1½ lb	2 lb
2 C all-purpose flour	2⅔ C all-purpose flour	3⅓ C all-purpose flour
¼ C whole wheat flour	⅓ C whole wheat flour	⅔ C whole wheat flour
2 T brown sugar	2½ T brown sugar	3 T brown sugar
⅜ C water	½ C water	⅝ C water
½ C milk	¾ C milk	⅞ C milk
1 T butter	1½ T butter	2 T butter
¼ C walnuts, chopped	⅓ C walnuts chopped	½ C walnuts chopped
1 tsp salt	1½ tsp salt	2 tsp salt
1½ tsp yeast	2 tsp yeast	2½ tsp yeast

1. Load and bake on the regular setting according to the instructions of your bread machine.
2. Serve plain, or while still warm, cover it with one of the Raisin Bread glazes (see page 47).

Miscellaneous Breads

Here are a few breads that don't seem to fit into any other category. They can be baked in the bread machine if you wish to do so.

French Spice Bread

This first recipe is something wonderful my wife created. It's flavorful, with an incredible fragrance when it's baking. Like the herb breads, you bake it instead of paying money for one of those air fresheners. Now, you can use the spices indicated below, her way; or you can try this: grind together, if you have a grinder for such things, 1 teaspoon each of cloves, nutmeg, and ginger; then add 1 tablespoon of ground cinnamon. It's called Spice Parisienne. Here's the bread recipe.

1 lb	1½ lb	2 lb
2¼ C bread flour	3 C bread flour	4 C bread flour
½ C milk	¾ C milk	⅞ C milk
¼ C water	⅜ C water	⅝ C water
1 T butter	1½ T butter	2 T butter
2 T brown sugar	2½ T brown sugar	3 T brown sugar
½ tsp nutmeg*	¾ tsp nutmeg*	1 tsp nutmeg*
½ tsp allspice*	¾ tsp allspice*	1 tsp allspice*
½ tsp ginger*	¾ tsp ginger*	1 tsp ginger*
1 tsp salt	1½ tsp salt	2 tsp salt
1½ tsp yeast	2 tsp yeast	2½ tsp yeast
¼ C plumped raisins**	¼ C plumped raisins**	¼ C plumped raisins**

*Or add the Spice Parisienne in the corresponding amounts: 1½ tsp, 2¼ tsp, or 3 tsp.
**Although we usually make it without raisins, they are an option. See instructions for plumping raisins on page 46.

Load and bake according to your machine's instructions on the rapid or regular setting. Then spread with one of the glazes below (my wife's contribution).

SIMPLE GLAZE I

¼ C confectioners' (10X) sugar   1 tsp milk

Mix well together and spread on a cooled loaf.

SIMPLE GLAZE II

Sprinkle confectioners' (10X) sugar on the loaf when it comes out of the pan.

Oatmeal Bread

Probably the first real, honest to goodness health bread. Unsurpassed for stick-toitiveness. It could be considered a whole-grain bread.

1 lb	1½ lb	2 lb
2 C bread flour	2½ C bread flour	3 C bread flour
¼ C oatmeal*	½ C oatmeal*	1 C oatmeal*
2 T brown sugar	2½ T brown sugar	3 T brown sugar
⅝ C water	⅞ C water	1 C water
¼ C milk	⅓ C milk	½ C milk
1 T butter	1½ T butter	2 T butter
1 tsp salt	1½ tsp salt	2 tsp salt
1½ tsp yeast	2 tsp yeast	2½ tsp yeast

*If you have cooked oatmeal left after breakfast, you can substitute it for the dry oatmeal without making any other changes in the recipe.

Load and bake on the rapid or regular setting.

Spicy Apple-Oatmeal Bread

1 lb	1½ lb	2 lb
2 C bread flour	2½ C bread flour	3¼ C bread flour
¼ C oatmeal	½ C oatmeal	¾ C oatmeal
2 T dark brown sugar	2½ T dark brown sugar	3 T dark brown sugar
½ C water	¾ C water	1 C water
¼ C milk	⅓ C milk	½ C milk
¼ C applesauce	⅓ C applesauce	½ C applesauce
1 T butter	1½ T butter	2 T butter
1 tsp cinnamon	1½ tsp cinnamon	2 tsp cinnamon
1 tsp salt	1½ tsp salt	2 tsp salt
2 tsp yeast	2½ tsp yeast	3 tsp yeast

Prepare as for Oatmeal Bread, above, adding the applesauce at the same time you add the rest of the liquids.

Potato Bread

When you drain the potato water prior to mashing the potatoes, save it in a jar in the refrigerator. You can use the leftover mashed potatoes as well. (Be sure to check the potato water each time before you use it if you save it in the refrigerator, because it spoils easily.) If you really must use instant potatoes, substitute 2 tablespoons of instant potato flakes for the real thing and use tapwater. See the variations below before mixing.

1 lb	1½ lb	2 lb
2¼ C all-purpose flour	3 C all-purpose flour	4 C all-purpose flour
⅞ C potato water	1⅛ C potato water	1½ C potato water
1 T sugar	1½ T sugar	2 T sugar
1 tsp salt	1½ tsp salt	2 tsp salt
2 T mashed potatoes	¼ C mashed potatoes	½ C mashed potatoes
1 T butter	2 T butter	3 T butter
1¼ tsp yeast	1½ tsp yeast	2 tsp yeast
½ tsp nutmeg*	½ tsp nutmeg*	½ tsp nutmeg*

*The nutmeg is optional; especially recommended if you're using the potato flakes.

Load all the ingredients and bake on the rapid or regular cycle.

Variations to Potato Bread

a. For **Whole Wheat Potato Bread,** substitute ¼ to ½ C of whole wheat flour for the an equal amount of the all-purpose flour and an equal amount of honey for the sugar.
b. For **Richer Potato Bread,** add 2 tablespoons of soy flour and 1 tablespoon of wheat germ; this will increase its protein and vitamin content (but don't tell the kids).
c. For **Garlic Potato Bread,** add 1 clove of pressed garlic, and substitute olive oil for the butter.
d. For **Ham and Potato Mustard Bread,** add 2 tablespoons Dijon-style mustard, or 1½ tablespoons Dijon mustard and ½ tablespoon coarse ground mustard; a good ½ teaspoon of fresh-ground black pepper; and some dried chopped onion; then the ham bits you have lying around in the refrigerator. A dandy bread to have with tomato soup. This is great for the meal in a loaf crowd.

Cinnamon Sugar Potato Bread

This is another of my wife's creations, heavily influenced by the Pennsylvania Dutch cooking to which she is inordinately drawn.

1 lb	1½ lb	2 lb
2¼ C flour	3 C flour	4 C flour
¼ C mashed potatoes	½ C mashed potatoes	¾ C mashed potatoes
¼ C whole milk	⅓ C whole milk	⅓ C whole milk
⅝ C water	⅞ C water	1⅛ C water
2 T brown sugar	2½ T brown sugar	3 T brown sugar
2 T butter	2½ T butter	3 T butter
1 tsp cinnamon	1½ tsp cinnamon	2 tsp cinnamon
1 tsp salt	1½ tsp salt	2 tsp salt
1½ tsp yeast	2 tsp yeast	2½ tsp yeast

Load and bake according to your machine's instructions on the rapid or regular setting, adding the mashed potatoes at the same time you add the liquids.

Peanut-Yogurt Bread

This is another of my wife's creations; you simply have to try it to believe it. She came up with it after buying a pound of crushed peanuts at a candy outlet in Altoona. You can chop the peanuts yourself in your food processor.

1 lb	1½ lb	2 lb
2¼ C flour	3 C flour	4 C flour
⅜ C water	½ C water	¾ C water
½ C plain yogurt	¾ C plain yogurt	1 C plain yogurt
1 T honey or sugar	2 T honey or sugar	2½ T honey or sugar
1 tsp salt	1½ tsp salt	2 tsp salt
1 T butter	1½ T butter	2 T butter
½ C chopped peanuts	¾ C chopped peanuts	1 C chopped peanuts
1½ tsp yeast	2 tsp yeast	2½ tsp yeast

Add the yogurt at the same time you add the rest of the liquids. Bake on the regular setting.

Thanksgiving Stuffing Bread

Of course, you can buy those expensive packages of stuffing mix. For that matter, you don't have to cook at all. But, if you really are serious about cooking that turkey for Thanksgiving or Christmas, or whenever you want to stuff a turkey or a chicken, well, you'll give thanks for this. This recipe will fit in all 3 bread machines, and yield a 1 lb loaf. Make it early enough to sit a few days before being used for stuffing.

1, 1½, or 2 lb

2 C all-purpose flour	¼ C whole wheat flour	1 T cornmeal
¼ C milk	⅝ C water	1 T butter
1 T brown sugar	1½ tsp salt	1 T poultry seasoning
1½ tsp yeast		

1. Put the ingredients into the bread pan, select the standard setting, and start.
2. When done, remove the loaf from the pan immediately and place it on a rack to cool.

If you're going to use it for stuffing, you can make this loaf a few days ahead to let it age. Or just go ahead and slice it and use it as a great sandwich bread for turkey, chicken, or pork sandwiches.

Thanksgiving Stuffing

What? You don't have a good recipe for stuffing? (I can't believe this.) This was enough to stuff a 17-lb bird, with some stuffing left over.

4 oz (1 stick) butter	1 C diced celery
1 C diced onion	1 apple, diced (optional)*
½ C raisins (optional)*	2 C water or chicken stock
1 loaf of Thanksgiving Stuffing Bread, diced into ½-inch pieces	lots of freshly ground black pepper
1 tsp salt	1 egg, lightly beaten

*If you're really bold, forget the apple and raisins and add one 6 oz can of oysters as your last ingredient.

Now, here's how: melt the butter in a large pan. Add the celery and onion, and sauté for maybe 5 minutes, until they are translucent; then add the apple and raisins if you're going to. Add the water or chicken stock; cook for a few minutes. Now add the bread cubes, pepper and salt, and mix thoroughly. Add the egg and oysters if you've got them, and mix that in well. Load the turkey and bake on.

OVEN-BAKED CREATIONS

The recipes in the next section of the book, Oven-Baked Creations, are made in the bread machine on the dough cycle and are removed from the bread machine after the first rising, kneaded and shaped by hand, allowed to rise, and then baked in the oven. This includes the chapters on Oven-Baked Breads; Rolls, Breadsticks and More; Sweet Rolls; Holiday Breads and Rolls; and Meals from the Bread Machine. (While some of the recipes could be baked in the bread machine, some won't have room to rise, especially in the 1 lb bread machine.)

The recipes indicate what sizes of bread machine will accommodate the ingredients. Where a recipe works best with certain amounts of ingredients, it was left at that ideal size, as noted. Make more than one batch of dough if you need more, in that case. The dough for many recipes can be prepared in more than one size of bread machine, as indicated in those recipes.

The Dough Setting

All yeast-risen bread and rolls are made from dough. And it is with the dough setting on your machine, or in your processor, mixer, whatever, that you make those long, round, flat, or even braided loaves, and the hundred or so different types of rolls and goodies that most of us can't be bothered to make any other way. On the dough setting of the bread machine, the initial mixing is done and the dough rises the first time in the bread machine. Then you take it out, punch it down, shape it, and let it rise outside the bread machine. What you can make is limited only by your imagination or the cookbook you're using.

Almost all bread machines have a dough setting. If you run into one of the old ones which doesn't have a dough setting, just pull the dough out of the machine after an hour or so. That goes for the newer ones too, should you change your mind when you have the makings in for bread and discover an hour later that what you really need is rolls for dinner.

The dough setting makes dough in an hour or so, depending upon the machine, and this is a handy way for you to time out your cooking. For instance, you can have things for breakfast you normally wouldn't consider, unless you like getting up at 4 a.m.; or dinner rolls that you forgot to buy and otherwise couldn't be bothered to make. You make your dough the night before, or even a day before, or before you go to work. On some of the newer machines, you can make dough using the timer, so it is ready when you want it. If your machine doesn't have this feature, make it earlier and leave it in the refrigerator until you need it. (Some machine even have a setting that tells you when to add raisins, nuts, etc., about 5 or 10 minutes before the end of the kneading cycle, but this isn't essential.)

Then you roll the dough out, or shape it, fill it with nuts and raisins, dates, cinnamon, sugar; do whatever you want with it, let it rise a bit, and then bake it. You can have rolls or loaves of bread, nice long baguettes, hot dog or hamburger rolls, cinnamon or sticky buns, Pompeiian bread (you never heard of that?); you name it. You'll probably soon love that dough setting and use it more and more. I believe the dough setting alone is probably worth the price of a bread machine. For as good as the bread is that is baked in a bread machine, hand-finished bread and rolls, baked in the oven, are still the best.

I almost always keep some dough in the fridge. After a day or two it becomes slightly sour—that's right, sourdough (more about this later).

Making pizza dough early in the day or the night before and leaving it in the fridge all day seems to contribute to a crispier crust. This was observed by our neighbor, Dave Parry, who teaches Philosophy at Penn State.

If you've never worked with dough before, you may be in for a surprise. The first time could be your last (if you don't read this section, that is). Just remember that people have been working with dough for thousands of years, so don't be afraid of it. And if you mess up, you can always toss it out, or at someone.

For you to understand what I mean, the best thing to do is make some dough, right now, in your bread machine. When it's ready, continue reading this.

Your dough should feel kind of soft, almost sticky, and even—well—alive. Strictly speaking it *is* alive. Ralph Pacifico, who owns a pretty good bakery in Altoona and has baked a loaf or two of bread in his time, says bread is the only thing man can bring to life.

The dough from your bread machine is as good or better than the dough we used to make before the machines. Dough can be sweet, savory, sour, or spicy; dark or light, rich or lean; but by and large it all feels pretty much the same. Certain kinds of weather are going to affect it. On a rainy or humid day, it will feel more sticky; on dry, cool days, it will be dryer and a bit harder to work. (You may need more liquid to get the same consistency on a dry day. If your dough feels too sticky, you may need to add a tablespoon or two more flour.) As you bake more, you'll get to know how the dough should feel. The machine does most of the work of kneading, an important subject we'll discuss next.

Kneading

Kneading, or working the dough, builds up the gluten in the dough. Gluten is a protein that forms in the endosperm of some grains. Wheat is the grain highest in gluten. Gluten is activated when flour is moistened, stirred well, and kneaded. (Rye, oats, corn, rice, barley, buckwheat, and bean flour don't have enough gluten to hold the bread together alone.) When liquid is added, gluten becomes the fibrous, rubbery stuff which, when combined with other items, makes dough. As the yeast you add to your ingredients grows and ferments, it produces carbon dioxide gas. The gluten fibers, strengthened by your kneading, trap this expanding gas, and this makes the dough rise.

Kneading helps determine the texture of the finished loaf. Fortunately or unfortunately, the machine does most of the kneading for you. I say "unfortunately" because over the centuries kneading has provided an excellent vent for anger and frustrations. Most recipes in the Oven-Baked Creations sections of this book require only a minute or two of kneading, more to get all the air out of the dough than to build up the gluten, which already was done for the most part in the bread machine on the dough cycle.

If you've never kneaded dough, let me explain how hand-kneading is done. When the dough cycle is done, first spread a little flour on a work surface.

Second, dump the dough onto it.

Third, push your hands onto and into the lump to press all the gas (good old carbon dioxide) that formed in rising out of the dough. The dough should be almost sticky. If it actually sticks to your hands and you can't work it, sprinkle a little more flour on it until it doesn't stick to your hands.

Fourth, flatten the lump into a round disc.

Fifth, and so on, fold the disc in half and press it flat again. Fold it in half again. Turn it over and repeat the process. Continue folding and flattening, for a minute or so. (Imagine having to do this for 10 or 12 minutes. That is what you would do if you were making bread without a bread machine.)

Sometimes the dough becomes too lively. It resists your kneading—in fact it becomes like a bunch of rubber, and you can't knead it at all. All you have to do is leave it alone—"let it rest," as they say—for about 5 to 10 minutes, which is usually all it takes. Then you can continue.

Raising Dough After the Dough Cycle

Almost all the books, and not just the bread machine books, say something to the effect of "let the rolls (or loaf) rise in a warm (90°F or 32°C), draft-free, place until it doubles in bulk." That gave me a guilty conscience for a while—was that space over by the stove really 90°F, and what about a draft? Someone was always coming into the kitchen. But I began to notice things: the dough left in the refrigerator overnight also rose. It sure wasn't 90°F in there, even with the kids in and out of it, and it sure wasn't draft-free. And was I sure it had doubled in bulk (that its volume was twice the original size)?

Your kitchen is probably warm enough for the dough to rise. If it is a bad winter, you can raise the dough in the warmed oven. About 90°F is warm enough. Turn on your oven to warm it for a minute or two; then turn it off again. Be sure to turn the oven off; then turn on the electric light in the oven, if your have one, and leave it on. Put the rolls or loaves in the oven and spray or sprinkle warm water on the loaves and in the oven—you're trying to make the humidity 80% or so. That will do nicely. Leave the bread in the oven for maybe a half-hour. Remove it from the oven and let it finish rising out of the oven. Check on it periodically. Meanwhile, set your oven to the desired temperature.

All the recipes in Oven-Baked Creations are to be mixed and kneaded and have the first rise in the bread machine on the dough cycle, then removed from the bread machine and baked in the oven. In fact, all the recipes in the preceding sections can have the dough prepared on the dough cycle and baked in the oven—you just have to take the risen dough out of the bread machine, shape the dough the way you want it, put it on a baking sheet or in some kind of pan, mold, tube pan, or no pan at all (you could even let the dough rise on a counter and bake it on quarry tiles on your oven shelf), let it rise, and bake it.

Oven-Baked Breads

Having read the preceding section on dough, you are ready to graduate to this section. If you're like me, this may be the section of the book you use most.

"Vienna" Bread

This was my father's favorite bread. He and I would sit down together with a loaf of fresh "Vienna" bread, a stick of butter, and a jar of Mrs. Dalton's Guava Jelly and not get up until we finished the bread. He never dieted, nor was he ever overweight—some people! This was 40 some years ago in Palm Beach. I don't think you can get Mrs. Dalton's Guava Jelly anymore, but Goya sells a good one. Don't forget the espresso. I don't think Dad ever had espresso. This recipe fits in all 3 sizes of bread machine on the dough cycle. Yield: one 14-inch loaf.

1, 1½, or 2 lb

1 egg white lightly beaten*	1 C water
2½ C unbleached all-purpose flour	1 T sugar
1 T lard or vegetable shortening**	1½ tsp salt
1½ tsp yeast	cornmeal for spreading on greased baking sheet

*Save the yolk and make it into egg wash for the glaze: mix it with 1 T water and a dash of salt.
**Some purists insist on corn oil.

1. Heat your oven to 400°F (205°C). Beat the egg white until it is foamy and add it to the rest of the ingredients.
2. Select the dough setting. Add all the ingredients except the egg yolk to the pan of the bread machine. Start the machine.
3. When the dough is done, remove it to a lightly floured surface. Roll the dough to an approximately 10 × 16 inch oblong; then fold the long sides over into a log-shaped loaf. Pinch the seam and ends closed.
4. On a baking sheet sprinkled with cornmeal, set the loaf, seam-side down. Sprinkle water on top. Let rise in a warm place until nearly doubled in bulk.
5. Brush with egg wash. Then, with a sharp knife or razor blade, make a cut about ¼ inch deep in the loaf top for the length of the log.
6. Bake in a 400°F oven for 25 to 30 minutes, until nice and brown. During the last 5 minutes, spray water on the bread and in the oven.

French Bread (Baguette)

Next is good old French bread, or the basic baguette. (Bet you're sorry you didn't pick up that baguette pan at that yard sale last summer.)

What you have here is the Basic Bread from the first section of the book, with just a few minor enhancements. When it's done, it should look like what you think of as real French bread. If you have a baguette pan, it should come out perfect. Also, one of these times, you may want to try making the dough a day or two before you want the bread, to let it sour a bit. This recipe fits in all 3 sizes of bread machine on the dough cycle. Yield: 1 long or 2 short baguettes (rod-shaped loaves).

1, 1½, or 2 lb

2½ C unbleached all-purpose flour	1 C water
1 T rye flour	2 tsp salt
1½ tsp yeast	cornmeal for the baking sheet

TOPPING (Optional)

1 egg yolk, beaten with 2 tsp water	poppy or sesame seeds

1. Load the ingredients in your machine (except the topping) and set it on the dough cycle. When the beeper sounds, remove the dough to a bowl, cover it, and let it rest for 30 minutes.
2. Dump it out onto a lightly floured surface. The dough may be rather wet and sticky. It's supposed to be. You may even want to wet your hands to handle the dough. Divide the dough into 2 equal portions (or make one long loaf; it depends on your oven). Use a rolling pin to roll each piece into an oblong about 4 to 5 inches wide, and maybe 14 to 16 inches long, and ¼ inch thick. Fold one long side over the other, press the sides together tightly, pinch the seam to seal it, and lay it, seam-side down on a cornmeal-covered cookie sheet (or the baguette pan, if you did pick it up at the yard sale). Taper the ends, pinching them to seal them.
3. Sprinkle or brush the top with water. Let the bread logs rise in a warm place until nearly doubled in bulk.
4. You can either leave the outsides plain or brush the tops with the egg wash topping and sprinkle with poppy or sesame seeds. Heat your oven to 500°F (260°C).
5. With a sharp knife or razor blade, make 3 or 4 cuts about ¼ inch deep diagonally across top of the risen bread logs. These are the "jets" that help excess gas to escape during baking.

6. Bake for 25 to 30 minutes or until golden brown in a 500°F (260°C) oven, with a pan of hot water in the bottom, or toss in some ice cubes after 5 minutes of baking. You want it to be done, and as Julia Child points out, maybe more done than less. You want a nice hard crust, after all.

Since French bread doesn't keep well, you may find yourself with leftover dry bread, and you can eat only so much French toast. Why not grind that dried bread up in your blender or processor and use it for bread crumbs? Try throwing in some herbs when you grind it up. This is what they charge you a couple of dollars for when you buy "seasoned bread crumbs" at the grocery store.

Italian Bread (New York Style)

If San Francisco gets an award for the best sourdough bread in the US, New York should get it for the best Italian bread. It seems to have consistently some of the best bread available in the country. The ovens are part of it; they're brick. But no small part is the demand, if not the desire, for really good bread. To get close to those great New York breads, try the following. The regular batch will fit in all 3 sizes of bread machine on the dough cycle. The large batch will fit in the 1½ or 2 lb machine. Yield: 1 lb (regular) or 1½ lb (large) loaf.

Regular (all sizes)	Large (1½ lb or 2 lb)
⅞ C water	1¼ C water
2¼ C unbleached all-purpose flour	3 C unbleached all-purpose flour
1 T whole wheat flour or rye	1 T + 1 tsp whole wheat flour or rye
1½ tsp salt	2 tsp salt
2 tsp brown sugar or honey	1 T brown sugar or honey
1 tsp vinegar	1½ tsp vinegar
1 T olive oil	1½ T olive oil
1½ tsp yeast	2 tsp yeast
cornmeal for baking sheet	cornmeal for baking sheet

TOPPING (for both sizes)

egg wash (1 egg beaten with 2 T water)

sesame seeds for top

1. Put all ingredients except the topping in the machine, and set it on the dough cycle. When the beeper sounds, remove the dough from the pan and put it into a bowl in the refrigerator to chill and rest for about 15 minutes.
2. Heat the oven to 400°F (205°C). Remove the dough to a lightly floured surface. Roll the dough to a 10 × 14 inch oblong; then fold the long sides over into a log-shaped loaf. Pinch the seams and ends closed.
3. On a baking sheet, sprinkle cornmeal. Set the loaf on it, seam-side down. Sprinkle water on top. Let it rise in a warm place until nearly doubled in bulk.
4. Brush with egg wash made of 1 egg beaten with 2 tablespoons of water. Sprinkle the top with sesame seeds. With a sharp knife, make 4 diagonal cuts, about ¼ inch deep, across the top.
5. Bake in a 400°F (205°C) oven for 25 to 30 minutes, until golden. During the last 5 minutes, spray water in the oven.

Pompeiian Bread

Did I tweak your interest when I mentioned this bread in the dough section? Where did I come up with this? Reading about Pompeii. It seems that in the 19th century, they found Pompeii, a city that had been buried by a volcanic eruption. When they began digging it up, they found the stuff of everyday life, like bread. Like Rome, Pompeii had lots of bakeries—they found lots of bread. It was stale, of course, but the loaves were whole. What interested me was the way the loaves were made. They were round and fairly flat, and were scored so wedges could be broken off to eat. We can do that.

Use the recipe for Italian Bread given above (steps 1 and 2), but shape the dough into a disc. Set the oven for 400°F (205°C).

3. On a baking sheet, sprinkle cornmeal. Set the loaf on it. Sprinkle water on top. Let rise in a warm place until nearly doubled in bulk.
4. Brush the bread with egg wash (see topping for Italian Bread). Sprinkle the top with sesame seeds. With a sharp knife, score the bread rather deeply right across the top into eight or twelve wedges, like cutting a pie.
5. Bake in a 400°F oven for 25 to 30 minutes, until golden. During the last 5 minutes, spray water in the oven or even on the bread.

Challah

This is the real thing, with that chewy texture, wonderful color, nearly sweet taste. This recipe is so good I make it in the bread machine as a regular loaf once or twice a week. The regular recipe will fit in all 3 sizes of bread machine on the dough cycle. The large recipe will fit in the 1½ or 2 lb machine. Yield: 1 lb (regular) or 1½ lb loaf (large).

Regular (all sizes)	Large (1½ or 2 lb)
1 egg + water to fill ⅞ C*	1 egg + water to fill 1⅛ C*
pinch of saffron**	pinch of saffon**
2¼ C all-purpose flour	3 C all-purpose flour
1½ T sugar	2 T sugar
1 T cooking oil	1½ T cooking oil
1 tsp salt	1½ tsp salt
1½ tsp yeast	2 tsp yeast
cornmeal for baking sheet	cornmeal for baking sheet

*Save 1 tsp for the topping.
**Optional. To color the Challah yellow, dissolve the saffron in the water about half an hour before using it.

TOPPING (both sizes)

1 tsp egg + water saved from ingredients

poppy seeds for sprinkling on top

1. Load all the ingredients except the cornmeal and topping into the bread machine and set on the dough cycle. When the beeper sounds, remove from the pan, knead the dough for a minute or two, and put it in a metal bowl. Place it in the refrigerator for 10 to 20 minutes. Set your oven to 360°F (183°C).
2. Remove the dough onto a lightly floured surface.
3. Divide the dough into three equal parts. Roll each part into a rope about 14 inches long (18 inches for the large recipe). Stretch them so the ends are skinnier than the middles.
4. Pinch the three strands together at one end and stretch the ropes out parallel. Now, just as if you were doing your daughter's hair, braid the ropes into a very loose braid (remember they are going to expand). Press the three loose ends together.
5. Spread cornmeal on a baking sheet. Put the braid on it. Let rise until double in bulk (about 50 minutes). Coat the loaf with egg wash and sprinkle on the poppy seeds.
6. At 360°F (183°C), bake 30 minutes, or until a wonderful, dark golden color.

Then again, you can simply put all ingredients in the bread pan, except the topping and cornmeal, and bake on the regular setting in the bread machine. You'll lose the texture, beauty, and poppy seeds, but that's all. It'll taste good and make great toast. This is also the basic recipe for a great Raisin Bread.

Monkey Bread

This is one of my wife's specialties, an interesting dinner or snack roll that was popular maybe 20 years ago. She first read about it in an article on barbecuing in some fancy cooking magazine. We have it often. It's fun to eat because you can just tear bits of it off. My wonderful wife usually laces it heavily with garlic. Sometimes she makes the sweet variation for a Sunday brunch or a treat with tea and coffee. You can use almost any dough—sweet, savory, or plain. I don't know where the name Monkey Bread comes from. One of our neighbors knew of it as "pinch bread." Nevertheless, it is the technique that makes it. The regular recipe will fit in all 3 sizes of bread machine on the dough cycle. The large recipe fits in the 1½ or 2 lb machine. Yield: 1 lb (regular) or 1½ lb (large) loaf.*

Basic Monkey Bread

Regular (all sizes)	Large (1½ or 2 lb)
2¼ C bread flour	3 C bread flour
⅝ C water	⅞ C water
¼ C milk	½ C milk
1 tsp shortening	1½ tsp shortening
1 T sugar	1½ T sugar
1 tsp salt	1¼ tsp salt
1½ tsp yeast	2 tsp yeast

*Note: you can use a loaf, fluted bundt pan, or tube pan.

FOR DIPPING (both sizes)

¼ to ½ C melted butter (or half butter, half margarine;
or half olive oil, half butter)

1. Put all ingredients except the dipping ingredients in the bread machine, and set it for the dough cycle. When the dough is done, dump it onto a lightly floured surface. Flatten it out and let it rest for a few minutes.
2. While it's resting, melt the dipping ingredients in a shallow saucepan.
3. Roll the dough to ¼ inch thickness.
4. Cut the dough into diamonds, or strips, or random shapes, and dip each

piece into the dipping. Distribute the pieces of dough evenly but haphazardly in the pan, forming irregular layers. We use an old fluted bundt pan. Set the oven to 350°F (177°C).

5. Let rise for ¾ of an hour, or until nearly doubled in bulk.
6. Bake in a 350°F oven for 30 minutes or until nice and brown. If it looks like the top is browning too quickly, put a piece of aluminum foil over it.
7. When done, dump the loaf onto a large platter. Pull off pieces as you go to eat them.

Sweet Variations for Monkey Bread

Use the Monkey Bread recipe above, but replace the water with half water and half milk, and increase the amount of sugar to 2 tablespoons for the 1½ lb loaf and 1½ tablespoons for the 1 lb loaf. Dip the dough pieces in melted butter; then roll them in a mixture of brown sugar and cinnamon. Place more melted butter, raisins and/or walnuts in between each layer, ending with more butter on top.

Instead of the raisins and walnuts, you can substitute two tablespoons of apple, butterscotch, or cherry filling (see the Danish recipes), or well-drained crushed pineapple in between each layer, ending with more butter on top. There is almost no end of things you can do.

Savory Variations for Monkey Bread

Use the basic Monkey Bread recipe, but add ½ teaspoon of garlic powder to the dry ingredients. When preparing the butter for dipping, sauté a couple of cloves of garlic in it. Sprinkle grated Parmesan or Romano cheese and crushed oregano between the layers.

Holly's Garlic Bread

This is a little something else my wife came up with. It is the technique that remarkable little woman has come up with that transforms this treat into something incredible. You have to serve it hot, and you have to make it like she does. It uses your basic white bread dough. The regular recipe will fit in all 3 sizes of bread machine on the dough cycle. The large recipe will fit in the 1½ or 2 lb machine. Yield: 1 lb loaf (regular) or 1½ loaf (large).

Regular (all sizes)	Large (1½ lb or 2 lb)
2¼ C bread flour	3 C bread flour
⅞ C water	1¼ C water
1 tsp salt	1¼ tsp salt
1 scant T sugar	1½ T sugar
1 tsp butter or oil	1½ tsp butter or oil
1½ tsp yeast	2 tsp yeast
1 T dried onions*	1½ T dried onions*
1 T Parmesan cheese*	1½ T Parmesan cheese*
Two 9-inch cake pans	Three 9-inch cake pans

*Optional

FOR GARLIC BUTTER (both sizes of Garlic Bread)

¼ C butter

2 cloves garlic

3 oz grated mozzarella

1. Load all the ingredients, except for the garlic butter, into the bread machine and set it on the dough cycle. When the beeper sounds, remove the dough from the pan onto a lightly floured surface. Press it down thoroughly and let it rest for a few minutes. Set the oven to 375°F (191 °C).
2. While the dough rests, melt ¼ cup of butter in a saucepan and sauté in it a couple of cloves of garlic. When nicely fragrant, remove the garlic and pour the melted butter into the 9-inch cake pans.
3. Then take about half the dough and, flattening it in your hands, press it into the cake pan, right on top of the garlic butter.
4. Sprinkle the grated mozzarella onto the top of the dough in the pan.
5. Let rise for only a few minutes.
6. Bake in a 375° F oven for 20 minutes or until nice and brown. The dough absorbs the butter, and the bread comes out nice and crisp and incredibly flavorful. Slice it into little wedges and serve.

My Own Sourdough Bread (Rob's Rye)

Here's how I make my mine. To many reasonable people this seems a bit silly. But it makes one good rye bread. Try it. You can bake it in any of the 3 sizes of bread machine.

Day One

½ C unbleached flour   ⅓ C warm water

1 tsp dry or regular whole milk   ¼ tsp yeast

Mix these ingredients well in a small mixing bowl (or even in the bread pan of your machine) and let them sit for a day, covered with a cloth (or out in the fog if you want to get authentic Bay Area sourdough).

Day Two

Add to the above ingredients, mixing well:

½ C rye flour   ¼ C warm water

Let the mixture sit for another day.

Day Three

Pour this starter mixture into the bread pan and add:

¼ C water   1 T olive oil

1½ tsp salt   1¼ C bread flour

1 scant tsp yeast   1 T dried onions, caraway
                                        seeds, 1 or 2 cloves of
Optional.   chopped garlic, etc.

At this point, decide whether you want to go ahead and bake it in the bread machine on the regular, rye, or whole wheat cycle, or prepare the dough on the dough cycle, let it age another day, coat it with an egg wash and poppy or sesame seeds, and bake it as a round loaf in your oven at 400°F (205°C) for 30 minutes.

Oven-Baked Sweet Loaves

This is another section full of loaves designed to have the first rise in the bread machine. Then you remove the dough from the machine, punch it down and knead it, shape it and let it rise, and bake it in the oven.

Banana Foster Bread

It's best to use those ripe, dark, ugly bananas. They are sweet and perfect for cooking—and usually on sale. Can be made in all 3 sizes of bread machine on the dough cycle. Yield: 1½ lb loaf.

Dough (1, 1½, or 2 lb)

3 C all-purpose flour	¼ C milk
1 egg	2 T butter
½ T brown sugar	1 tsp salt
½ tsp cardamom	¼ tsp cinnamon
1½ tsp yeast	1 ripe banana, mashed, and water to fill ¾ cup

FOR THE SAUCE

2 T butter	½ C brown sugar
1 T banana liqueur or brandy	1 ripe banana

1. Load the bread pan with all the ingredients except the sauce, and select the dough setting of your machine.
2. When done, remove the dough to a greased bowl. Cover it and let it sit in the refrigerator until chilled—or overnight.
3. For the sauce, cut the banana in half and then into long thin slices. Melt the butter in a saucepan, add the brown sugar and liqueur, and cook over medium heat to form a nice syrup, stirring gently. Add the banana and cook for a few more minutes. Let the sauce cool to a warm room temperature.
4. Roll out the dough to a thin oblong about 12 × 16 inches.
5. Spread the Foster sauce and bananas onto the oblong. Now fold the long sides over the sauce into a log, pinch the seams and ends tightly, and place it in a regular loaf pan, seam-side down. Set your oven to 360°F (183°C). Let the dough rise in a warm place for about an hour.
6. Bake in a 360°F (183°C) oven for about 30 to 40 minutes. Serve hot.

Rolled Raisin Breakfast Loaf

This is my "special occasion" raisin bread recipe, and may become yours. It is more involved than the regular raisin bread recipes, but it is worth every extra minute you have to spend on it. Yield: 1½ lb loaf. The ingredients will fit in all three sizes of bread machine on the dough cycle.

Dough (1, 1½, or 2 lb)

2 C all-purpose flour	1 C whole wheat flour
¾ C liquid*	¼ C milk
1 egg	2 T butter
2 T brown sugar	1 tsp salt
1½ tsp yeast	

FILLING

½ C raisins	¼ C brandy or dark rum
½ C brown sugar	4 T butter, really soft
1 tsp cinnamon	¼ tsp ground cloves
¼ tsp ground nutmeg	

GLAZE

½ C confectioners' sugar	2 tsp milk
2 drops of vanilla	1 pinch of salt

*See Step 1.

1. Before you do anything else, measure ¾ cup of water into a microwave-safe bowl and add ¼ cup of brandy or dark rum to the water. Now put the raisins in the bowl, and the bowl into the microwave. Cook them for about 1 minute on high. After a few minutes, drain the liquid off, but save it and let the water–rum mixture cool. Use it as the liquid in the dough recipe.
2. Load the bread pan with all the ingredients for the dough, and select the dough setting.
3. When the dough is ready, remove it from the pan, place it in a greased bowl, and chill in the refrigerator for ½ hour.
4. On a lightly floured surface, roll the dough into a 10 × 15 inch oblong.
5. Let the dough rest while you mix the raisins with the sugar and spices for the filling.
6. Spread the softened 4 tablespoons of butter on the oblong; then spread the raisins with the sugar–spice mixture on the buttered oblong. Press the raisin mixture into the dough, either with your hands or with a rolling pin. This stops the layers from separating when the loaf bakes. Roll the oblong into a log; pinch the seams and ends closed.

7. Lay the log on a greased baking sheet, with the seam down. Let it rise. (If you do this the night before, let the log rise in the refrigerator overnight.)
8. Bake in a 350 °F (177°C) oven for 35 minutes or until done.
9. Mix the glaze ingredients and spread it on the bread while it is still warm.

Rolled Raisin Breakfast Loaf Two

This is a tasty, but different, loaf from the above. I submit it because one could conceivably grow tired of the previous one. Yield: 1¼ lb loaf; will fit in all 3 sizes of bread machine on the dough cycle.

Dough (1, 1½, or 2 lb)

2½ C all-purpose flour	1 egg
¾ C water (see Step 1)	jigger of brandy or dark rum
1 T lemon juice	1 tsp grated lemon zest
2 T brown sugar	1½ T corn oil
½ tsp cardamom	1 tsp salt
1½ tsp yeast	

FOR THE FILLING

½ C of raisins	½ C brown sugar
4 T soft whipped butter	1 tsp cinnamon
¼ tsp ground cloves	

1. Prepare the raisins and water–rum mixture as in Step 1 of the Rolled Raisin Breakfast Loaf.
2. Load the bread pan with all the ingredients for the dough, and select the dough setting. When the dough is done, remove it from the pan, place it in a bowl, and chill it in the refrigerator for ½ hour.
3. On a lightly floured surface, roll the dough into a 10 × 15 inch oblong.
4. Let the dough rest while you mix together the raisins, ½ cup sugar, and spices for the filling.
5. Spread the softened butter on the dough oblong; then sprinkle the sugar–spice–raisin mix over the butter. Press all this into the dough, either with your hands or with a rolling pin. This stops the layers from separating when the loaf bakes. Starting on one long side, roll the dough into a log. Pinch the seam and ends closed.
6. Put it in a greased baking pan. (I use the heat-resistant Pyrex loaf pan my daughter gave me.) Let the dough rise. (If you do this the night before, let the log rise in the refrigerator overnight.)
7. Bake in a 350°F (177°C) oven for 35 to 40 minutes, or until done.

Rolls, Breadsticks, and More

Sandwich Rolls (or Hamburger Buns, or Hot Dog Rolls, or . . .)

Let's begin at the beginning with Sandwich Rolls or Hamburger Buns, the generic name for those all-purpose round rolls. They're quick and easy, and you can make them any size you want. Or you can make hot dog rolls. Wouldn't it be great to find those foot-long hot dogs and make the rolls to fit?

Make them in the afternoon when you discover that you're out of hamburger buns and you want hamburgers (or hot dogs, or any kind of sandwich) for dinner. Actually, you can use almost any savory bread recipe in the book, but to save you turning more pages, try this one. It's designed to be done on the dough cycle. The regular recipe yields 8 rolls. The large recipe yields 12 rolls. Both fit in all 3 sizes of bread machine. The banquet size recipe yields 15 rolls and fits in the 1½ lb and 2 lb bread machine.

Regular (all sizes)	Large (all sizes)	Banquet (1½ and 2 lb)
2¼ C bread flour	3 C bread flour	4½ C bread flour
⅜ C water	¾ C water	6 oz water
½ C milk	½ C milk	1 C milk
1 T butter	1½ T butter	2 T butter
1 T sugar	1½ T sugar	2 T sugar
1 tsp salt	1½ tsp salt	2 T salt
1½ tsp yeast	2 tsp yeast	3 tsp yeast

TOPPING (all sizes)

1 egg, beaten +2 T water and a pinch of salt

¾ T poppy or sesame seeds (optional)

1. Load the bread pan with all the ingredients except the topping. Select the dough cycle and start the machine.
2. When the beeper sounds, remove the dough to a bowl; cover it with plastic wrap and rest it in the refrigerator until needed; or empty the dough onto a floured surface and let it rest for 5 to 10 minutes.
3. Then divide the dough into 8, 12, or 15 equal portions, depending on the size of your dough batch, and roll each portion into a ball. Flatten each ball to about ½ inch thick with the palm of your hand, stretching it from the middle to the edges. Put the flattened balls on a cookie sheet that is greased

or has cornmeal sprinkled on it. Leave space between the circles for the dough to expand as it rises.

4. Sprinkle water on top. Let the dough rise in a warm place until nearly doubled (45 minutes, usually).
5. Brush the rolls with the beaten egg and sprinkle with poppy seeds or sesame seeds if desired. Bake in a 350°F (177°C) oven for 20 minutes or until golden brown. Let the rolls cool before slicing.

VARIATIONS

Hot Dog Buns: shape into a long oval shape instead of the round shape.
Steak Sandwich Buns: shape into a long, wide ovals.

Parker House Rolls

These are my pick for the quintessential dinner roll. Outside of cities with good bakeries, good Parker House Rolls are hard to find—until now, of course. They show up in some bread machine books with a recipe similar to the one above. But that's not them. They aren't Parker House Rolls, unless they taste, look, and feel, like Parker House Rolls. For those who remember, or those who have never tasted them, here they are. Can be made in all 3 sizes of bread machine. Yield: about 20 rolls.

1, 1½, or 2 lb

2½ C all-purpose flour	1 egg
¾ C water	1 T lard or shortening
1½ tsp salt	2 T sugar
1 T butter	¾ tsp yeast

1. Load the bread machine with all the ingredients and choose the dough cycle.
2. When the beeper sounds, remove the dough to a floured surface. Push the air out of the dough, let it rest 10 minutes, and then roll out the dough to be ⅜ inch thick. With a biscuit cutter, cut it into 3-inch circles, and brush the tops with melted butter. Fold each in half, creasing it with the handle of a butter knife, and place them, not quite touching, on a greased baking sheet. Heat your oven to 400°F (205°C).
3. Let them rise for about 30 minutes. Then bake for 15 minutes in the 400°F oven.
4. Now here is *the* important touch: When you remove the rolls from the oven, slide them from the baking sheet onto the counter. Coat the tops with butter; then cover the rolls with a kitchen towel as they cool. And that's how you make Parker House Rolls!

Simple Butter Dinner Rolls

These are probably what most people have in mind when they think of good dinner rolls. You can make these as simple round rolls, braid them, or make them up as cloverleaf rolls. On the dough cycle, the small recipe yields 9 rolls and fits into all 3 sizes of bread machine. The large recipe fits in the 1½ lb and 2 lb machine and yields 15 rolls. The banquet recipe fits in the 2 lb machine and yields 18 rolls.

Small (all sizes)	Large (1 ½ lb or 2 lb)	Banquet (2 lb)
2¼ C all-purpose flour	3 C all-purpose flour	4½ C all-purpose flour
½ C milk	¾ C milk	1 C milk
⅜ C water	½ C water	6 oz water
1 T sugar	1 T + 1 tsp sugar	2 T sugar
½ tsp salt	1 scant tsp salt	1 tsp salt
3 T butter	4 T butter	6 T butter
1½ tsp yeast	2 tsp yeast	3 T yeast

FOR BRUSHING ON TOP (all sizes): melted butter

1. Load the bread pan with all the ingredients except the extra tablespoon of butter; select the dough setting.
2. When the beeper sounds, remove the dough to a bowl. Cover. Rest the dough in the refrigerator until needed, or overnight.
3. The following are some roll shapes you can make.
   a. Roll out the dough on a lightly floured surface into a "rope." Cut it into equal pieces. Place them on a greased cookie sheet, let them rise, and make a cut down the middle of each about ¼ inch deep.
   b. Cut the "rope" and divide it into pieces 6 to 8 inches long; tie each into a simple loose knot. Place them on a greased cookie sheet.
   c. Cut the rope into 1- or 2-inch little balls; put three each into a muffin tin to make cloverleaf rolls. You can also think up some shapes yourself.
4. Sprinkle water on top and let the rolls rise at 90°F (32°C) for 20 to 30 minutes, or until doubled in bulk.
5. Brush the top of the rolls with the extra butter; bake at 360°F (183°C) for 15 to 20 minutes, or until golden brown.
6. Serve hot or cold.

English Muffins

Yes, English muffins! And better even than the best you can buy. (You'll have to wonder why they're so expensive in the store.) Actually, it is the technique more than the dough that makes the English muffin. I have made them using leftover Parker House Roll dough—were they something! You can use pretty much what you have around. This recipe is close to what you're familiar with, but better, of course. Easiest when you make the dough the night before. This recipe fits in all 3 sizes of bread machine. Yield: 8.

1, 1½, or 2 lb

½ C milk	1½ T butter
⅜ C water	1½ tsp malt vinegar
1 egg	2¼ C all-purpose flour
1 T sugar	1 tsp salt
1 tsp yeast	1 C cornmeal
oil for skillet	

1. Warm the milk and butter until the butter melts.
2. Add the water and vinegar.
3. Put this liquid into the bread pan of your bread machine.
4. Add the egg, slightly beaten.
5. Add the all-purpose flour, sugar, salt, and then the yeast.
6. Select the dough setting on your machine, and start it.
7. When the beeper sounds, remove the dough to a bowl. Cover with plastic wrap. Let the dough rest in the refrigerator for at least 30 minutes, or overnight.
8. When you are ready to bake the muffins, put the cornmeal into a separate bowl. With a large serving spoon and your hand, take out a half cup of the dough. Shape it into a round ball and roll it in the cornmeal; then flatten the ball into a ½-inch thick, 4 inch wide circle.
9. Place the circles on a piece of waxed paper where it is fairly warm. Let them rest for 10 minutes.
10. Put some oil on a medium-hot skillet. (I use a 12-inch cast iron skillet.) Place three or four at a time, or as many as will fit, on the skillet. After a couple of minutes, flip them over. Lower the heat, and cook them covered, flipping them at 3- or 4-minute intervals, for a total cooking time of 15 minutes.
11. When done, let them cool. Use a fork to separate them, pull them apart, and toast them. That's all there is to it.

Open Books

Open Books—that's what I call these things. They separate nicely and look like an open book, pages and all. They're another of those things, like Monkey Bread, with all sorts of interesting variations. You can make them as described below and have a delightful, fluffy dinner roll. Or, when you get to step #6, start putting other stuff on with the butter: chopped chives and garlic, for example. Having chicken? Spread a little poultry seasoning. Want them for breakfast? Spread sugar and cinnamon; you get the idea. Can be made in all 3 sizes of bread machine. Yield: 6 or 8. Recipe can be doubled to make 12 or 15.

1, 1½, or 2 lb

¾ C milk	1 T lard or vegetable shortening
1½ T sugar	¾ tsp salt
2½ C all-purpose flour	¼ C water
1 tsp yeast	½ lb tub of whipped butter at room temperature, or soft

1. Heat the milk in a saucepan; then add the lard, the sugar, and salt. Stir and let dissolve in the pan. Pour into the bread pan of the bread machine. Then add the water.
2. Measure the flour into the bread pan.
3. Put the bread pan in bread machine, select the dough setting, and start.
4. When the beeper signals that the dough is ready, remove it to a greased bowl. Cover and put it in the refrigerator until thoroughly chilled (an hour).
5. Remove to a lightly floured surface. Roll out into a nearly perfect rectangle, ¼ inch thick.
6. Important! Spread or dot the butter lightly on ⅔ of the rectangle. Fold the third that isn't buttered into the ⅔ that is; then fold the remaining buttered third over the unbuttered third. You should now have three layers.
7. Now turn this layered piece a quarter turn, east to south, as they say, and roll it out as thin as you can. Repeat step #6, then step #7 again. It should look like a square. Put it in the fridge and let it chill for 30 minutes or so. Preheat the oven to 400°F (205°C). Take it out of the fridge and do the same thing again, maybe twice more—depends on how many pages you want. (If the dough starts getting lively, hard to work, and resists your rolling, in between the buttering steps, put it back in the fridge.)
8. Now, when you roll out the dough, make it either square, maybe an 8 inch square, or a long narrow rectangle 4 × 16 inches long, whichever's easier. Cut strips 2 inches wide. Then cut the strips into 4-inch lengths. What you are aiming for is strips of dough 2 × 4 inches.

9. Fold these strips in half and put each in the cup of a lightly greased muffin tin. Spread a little soft whipped butter on each of the rolls and put them into a preheated 350°F (177°C) oven and bake 20 to 25 minutes. You'll love them!

Sesame Onion Board

Seeing a complex recipe for Sesame Onion Board recently, my wife recalled having read the following recipe 20 years ago. She possesses an uncanny skill at duplicating recipes from memory—or even from the ingredients panel on the sides of packages. This Sesame Onion Board is good with beer out on the deck—with soups, too. This recipe fits in all 3 sizes of bread machine. Yield: one 1¼ lb loaf.

1, 1½, or 2 lb

2½ C all-purpose flour	1 T sugar
1 C water	1 tsp onion salt
1 tsp dried minced onion	1 T grated onion
¼ tsp pepper	1 tsp yeast
1½ T olive oil or 1 T sesame oil	cornmeal for the baking sheet

TOPPING

1 egg yolk beaten with 2 tsp water	1 T dried minced onion
1 T sesame seeds	

1. Load the bread pan of your bread machine with all the ingredients except the cornmeal and the topping, set it for the dough cycle, and start it.
2. When the dough is done, remove it from the pan into a greased bowl and place it in the refrigerator for ½ hour. Set your oven to 375°F (191°C).
3. Move the dough to a lightly floured surface. Roll the dough out to a thin rectangle that will fit on your baking sheet. Sprinkle your baking sheet with cornmeal and transfer the dough rectangle to it.
4. Make lengthwise shallow cuts with a serrated knife down the dough at about ½-inch intervals.
5. Sprinkle water on top. Let the dough rise in a warm place for 30 minutes.
6. Brush the rectangle of dough with the egg-and-water topping. Sprinkle the top of the dough with sesame seeds and dried onion.
7. Bake in a 375°F oven for 25 to 30 minutes, until golden brown.

Crescents (Croissants)

Feel daring? Don't let the long directions put you off. Remember, once you've done them, you've done them, and they become easy to do. They're worth it. Yield: 6 or 8 croissants. The dough will fit in all 3 sizes of bread machine.

1, 1½, or 2 lb

¾ C water	1 T lard
1½ T sugar	¾ tsp salt*
¼ C milk	2½ C bread flour**
1 tsp yeast	½ lb tub of whipped butter at room temperature

*Use ¾ tsp of salt if you are using salted butter in Step #6. Use 1 tsp if you are using unsalted butter.
**You can use all-purpose flour, but they won't rise as high.

1. If your bread machine doesn't preheat, then heat the water, lard, sugar, and salt in a saucepan, and stir to dissolve. Add the milk to cool it, and put it in the bread pan of the bread machine.
2. Measure the flour into the bread pan.
3. Put the bread pan in the bread machine, select the dough setting, and start it.
4. When the beeper signals that the dough is ready, remove the dough from the bread pan to a greased bowl. Refrigerate, covered, until thoroughly chilled (an hour).
5. Remove to a lightly floured surface. Roll out as thin as you can into a nearly perfect rectangle.
6. Spread or dot the butter lightly on two-thirds of the rectangle (figure a). Then fold the third that isn't buttered onto the two-thirds that is (figure b); then fold the remaining buttered third over the unbuttered third (figure c). You should now have three layers. If you don't, you've seriously miscounted.
7. Now turn this layered piece a quarter turn, east to south, and roll it out as thin as you can again. Repeat Step #6, and put the whole thing on a plate, covered, in the fridge. After an hour or so, repeat steps #6 and #7 again. Then do it one more time. If the dough starts getting lively, hard to work, and resists your rolling, in between the buttering steps, let it sit for 5 minutes.
8. After doing the above, put the dough back in the fridge and let it rest for at least a half-hour. Remove from the refrigerator and roll it out again.
9. This time, rolling out the dough, try for a long, narrow, maybe 6 × 16 inch strip of dough. Now, trim off the rounded edges on all four sides until you have an approximately 5 × 15 inch rectangle (figure d). Cut this into three nearly perfect squares (figure e). Cut these squares in half diagonally. You should have six equilateral triangles.

10. Roll these triangles, starting with the wide side and stretching slightly as you roll (figure f), and shape them into the familiar crescent rolls (figure g).

11. Place the rolls on a lightly greased baking sheet and chill them for a half-hour. You don't want them to rise this time. Spread a little of the soft whipped butter on the top of each of the rolls and put them into a preheated 400°F (205°C) oven. After 10 minutes, reduce the heat to 350°F (177°C) and bake until they are golden—another 10 to 15 minutes. That's all there is to it.

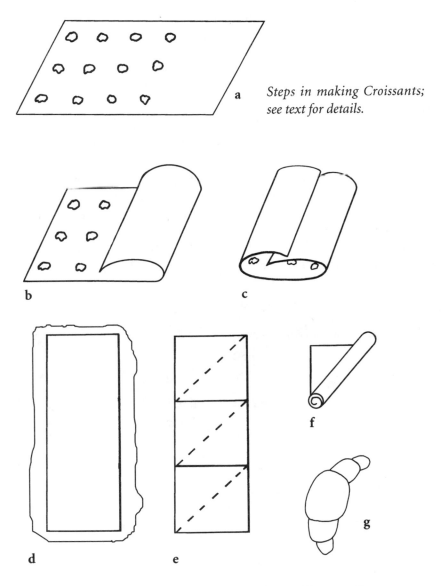

Steps in making Croissants; see text for details.

Breadsticks

Breadsticks are necessary with soup, stew, or chowder. Here are some of the ways we make them. But you can make them with almost any kind of bread dough, and make them fatter or thinner, longer or shorter, crispier or breadier, as you like. This recipe will fit in all 3 sizes of bread machine; you can double it, if you wish, but the doubled recipe will not fit in the 1 lb bread machine. Yield: 12 to 24 breadsticks, depending on the size you make them.

Basic Breadsticks
1, 1½, or 2 lb

1⅛ C water	3 C bread flour
2 tsp salt	1 tsp yeast

1. Load the bread pan with the ingredients, select the dough setting, and start the machine.
2. When the dough is done, set your oven to 450°F (232°C). Remove the dough to a floured surface.
3. Divide the dough into pieces about the size of a golf ball. Roll each piece into a stick about 8 inches long and the diameter of your little finger.
4. Lay the sticks on a cookie sheet sprinkled with cornmeal, about an inch apart. Spritz with water.
5. Immediately bake in a 450°F oven for about 10 to 15 minutes. Eat them with Manhattan clam chowder and beer.

Bready Breadsticks

These have a soft, breadlike consistency.

1, 1½, or 2 lb

⅜ C water	1 T sugar
½ C milk	1 tsp salt
2¼ C bread flour	1 T butter or oil
1 tsp yeast	¼ C grated cheese*
1 T dried minced onion*	1 T grated Parmesan cheese*
*Optional.	

TOPPING

1 beaten egg white	1 T poppy seeds, sesame seeds, or coarse salt

1. Load the bread pan with all the ingredients except the topping; select the dough setting; start the machine.
2. When the dough is done, remove it to a bowl; cover it with plastic wrap and let it rest in the refrigerator.
3. Divide the dough in half and roll it out to about ½-inch thick. Cut the dough into strips about 8 × 2 inches. Roll each strip into a tube shape and transfer them to cookie sheets, leaving space between them for rising. Sprinkle water on top.
4. Let them rest in a warm place for 10 to 15 minutes. Heat the oven to 400°F (205°C).
5. Brush the sticks with egg white and sprinkle them with poppy seeds, sesame seeds, or coarse salt.
6. Bake in a 400°F oven for 15 minutes or until golden brown. Cool on a rack.

Quick Breadsticks

1. Prepare either of the recipes for breadsticks, but roll the dough out to about ½ inch thick, cut into ½-inch wide strips, and put them on cookie sheets with a sprinkling of cornmeal.
2. Brush with the egg plus water mixture (topping) and sprinkle with poppy or sesame seeds.
3. Proceed as with either of the above recipes. These won't be quite as attractive as the rolled variety, but they taste as good and cut the preparation time in half.

Bagels

If your town is not blessed with a good bagel baker, you can use this recipe, or for that matter, you can use any one of several dough recipes. (The Challah recipe works very nicely for egg bagels.) It is, after all, the technique that makes them. You will need good unbleached all-purpose flour and a little extra gluten for best results. Also, you might want to pick up a jar of malt (liquid or powder) at a health food store; use it in place of sugar—it makes a better crust. After the first time you make bagels, you'll see it's pretty easy. The small batch fits in all 3 machines. The large batch fits in the 1½ or 2 lb machine. Yield: small batch, 6 to 8 bagels; large batch, 12 to 15 bagels.

Small batch (1, 1½, or 2 lb)	Large batch (1½ or 2 lb)
2½ C all-purpose flour*	5 C all purpose flour*
1 tsp sugar (or 2 of malt)	2 tsp sugar (or 1 T of malt)
1 C water	1¾ C water
1 tsp salt	2 tsp salt
1 tsp yeast	1½ tsp yeast

*Replace 1 T of the flour with gluten, if you have it.

TOPPING (both sizes)

1 egg, beaten with 2 tsp water and a pinch of salt

poppy seeds, sesame seeds, or pretzel salt (optional)

1. Load the bread pan of the bread machine with the ingredients, except the topping. Select the dough cycle and start the machine.
2. When the dough is done, either let the dough rest in a greased bowl for 10 minutes or keep it in the refrigerator to chill for a half-hour. It will be even easier to use.
3. Divide the dough into 6 or 8 equal portions, each about the size of a small tangerine, for the smaller recipe or 12 to 15 portions for the large batch. Put a little flour on your hands; then flatten and stretch each portion on a lightly floured surface. Stick your finger in the middle of each and stretch it into a circle with a 2-inch hole in the middle, turning the dough so the inside of the circle is on the outside.
4. Place the bagels on waxed paper sprinkled with cornmeal. Spray water on top, and let them rest in a warm place for 30 minutes.
5. Bring 3 quarts of water to a boil. Reduce to a simmer, *making sure the water is still boiling when you place the bagels into it.* Cook 3 or 4 bagels at a time for 1 minute on each side. Remove with a slotted spoon and drain.

6. Place on a baking sheet sprinkled with cornmeal; brush them with the egg and water topping mixture. Sprinkle them with poppy or sesame seeds, or just leave them plain if you prefer.

7. Bake in a 475°F (245°C) oven for 20 minutes, or until the crust is golden brown and crisp.

VARIATIONS

Raisin Bagels: Add ¼ cup plumped raisins to the dough. (See p. 46 for plumping raisins.)

Onion Bagels: Add 2 tablespoons minced onions to the dough.

Garlic Bagels: Add garlic powder or a couple of crushed cloves of garlic to the dough.

You can make whole wheat, egg, or other kinds of bagels; the technique is the same.

Before we leave this section, here are a couple of ideas for rolls you may want to try. When you get right down to it, dinner rolls are just little loaves of bread, which means, of course, you can make your rolls out of anything you want. Here are two more I make often.

Really Basic Dinner Rolls

This recipe will fit in all 3 sizes of bread machine. Yield: 8 or 10 rolls.

1, 1½, or 2 lb

2½ C all-purpose flour	1 C water
1 tsp sugar	1½ tsp salt
1 tsp oil	1½ tsp yeast
cornmeal for the baking sheet	

1. Load the bread pan of your bread machine with all the ingredients except the cornmeal. Select the dough cycle and start the machine.
2. When the beeper sounds, remove the dough to a floured surface. Set the oven to 400°F (205°C). Let the dough rest for 5 to 10 minutes; then divide the dough into 8 to 10 equal portions and roll each portion into a ball. Put the balls on a cookie sheet that has been greased or sprinkled with cornmeal. Leave space between the balls for rising.
3. Sprinkle water on top. Let them rise in a warm place until nearly doubled; 30 minutes will do.
4. Bake in a 400°F oven for 25 minutes or so, or until done.

Roman Stones

My wife insists I include these. When done, they look like stones that came out of the Tiber (or the Susquehanna, for that matter). They are greyish, a bit salty, but soft and chewy, with a hard crust. This recipe will fit in all 3 sizes of bread machine. Yield: 8 to 10 portions.

1, 1½, or 2 lb

2½ C all-purpose flour	1 T whole wheat flour
1 T rye flour	1 C water
1 tsp honey	1½ tsp salt
1 tsp oil	1 tsp yeast
cornmeal for the baking sheet	

1. Load the bread pan of your bread machine with all the ingredients except the cornmeal. Select the dough cycle. Start the machine.
2. When the beeper sounds, remove the dough to a floured surface. Set the oven for 425°F (218°C). Let the dough rest for 5 to 10 minutes; then divide the dough into 8 to 10 equal portions and roll each portion into a ball. Put the balls on a cookie sheet that has been greased or sprinkled with cornmeal. Leave space between them for rising.
3. Sprinkle water on top. Let them rise in a warm place until nearly doubled; 30 minutes will do.
4. Bake in a 425°F oven for 25 minutes or so, or until done.

Sweet Rolls

Here is another batch of recipes for which you prepare the dough in your bread machine on the dough cycle, then briefly knead by hand, let the dough have its second rise outside of the bread machine, and bake in the oven.

Cinnamon Buns

Yes, those little morsels they sell for too much money—and which don't taste nearly as good as yours will. Will fit in all 3 sizes of bread machine. Yield: 12.

Dough for 1, 1½, or 2 lb

2½ C all-purpose flour	2 T sugar
¾ C milk	1 egg + water to fill ¼ C
1 tsp salt	3 T butter
1½ tsp yeast	

FILLING

1 (rounded) tsp cinnamon	⅓ C brown sugar
2 T melted butter	¼ C chopped raisins
1 egg, beaten	

VANILLA FROSTING FOR CINNAMON BUNS

½ C confectioners' sugar	1¼ tsp milk
¼ tsp vanilla extract	

1. Load the bread pan of the bread machine with the ingredients (except the filling and frosting), select the dough cycle, and start the machine. When the dough is done, remove it to a greased bowl. Cover the dough and let it rest in the refrigerator for 30 minutes, or overnight if you prefer.
2. Roll out the dough on a lightly floured surface into a 10 × 16 inch rectangle. Spread with the melted butter; sprinkle with a mixture of the brown sugar and cinnamon, then raisins. Roll the dough up, jelly-roll fashion, into a 16-inch log. Seal the edge with beaten egg. Slice the log into 12 equal portions.
3. Place the slices in a 9 × 13 inch pan so they are not touching. Spritz with water. Let rise in a warm place for 30 minutes or until nearly doubled. Brush the rolls with the remaining beaten egg.
4. Bake in a 360°F (183°C) oven for 15 to 20 minutes, or until lightly browned. Place the pan on a rack to cool.
5. To make the frosting, mix the confectioners' sugar with the milk until all the sugar is dissolved. Spread the rolls with the vanilla frosting and serve.

Pennsylvania Dutch Sticky Buns

Similar to the Cinnamon Bun recipe, but much stickier; beloved in central and eastern Pennsylvania. Fits in all 3 sizes of bread machine. Yield: 12.

Dough for 1, 1½, or 2 lb

2½ C all-purpose flour	2 T sugar
¾ C milk	1 egg plus water to fill ¼ C
1 tsp salt	3 T butter
1½ tsp yeast	

FILLING

1 rounded tsp cinnamon	⅓ C brown sugar
1 egg, beaten	

TOPPING

2 T butter	½ C brown sugar
¼ C walnuts, pecans, and raisins	

1. Load the bread pan of the bread machine with the dough ingredients. Select the dough cycle, and start the machine. When the dough is done, remove it to a greased bowl. Cover the dough and let it rest in the refrigerator for 30 minutes or overnight.
2. Roll out the dough on a lightly flowered surface into a 10 × 16 inch rectangle. Sprinkle the dough with a mixture of the brown sugar and cinnamon from the filling ingredients. Roll the dough up jelly-roll fashion into a 16-inch log. Seal the edge with beaten egg. Slice the log into 12 equal portions.
3. In a 9 × 13 inch baking pan, melt 2 tablespoons of butter, add to it ½ cup of brown sugar and ¼ cup walnuts, pecans and/or raisins, and spread over the bottom of the pan. This will become the topping. (The buns are baked upside down in the same way that an upside down cake is baked.) Place the slices together in the pan with the sides nearly touching. Set the oven for 360°F (183°C). Sprinkle the buns with water. Let them rise at 90°F (32°C) for 20 to 30 minutes, or until nearly doubled. Brush the buns with the remaining beaten egg.
4. Bake in a 360°F oven for 15 to 20 minutes, or until brown.
5. Immediately turn the buns out of the pan, right-side up. Serve hot, tepid, or cool.

Potato Doughnuts

My wife actually made this up while trying to duplicate those wonderful potato doughnuts we used to see in our area. As Christmas neared, she found in her collection of holiday recipes the recipe for the French Canadian croquignoles. It was virtually identical to this, except the croquignoles were cooked as little rectangles. They are billed as a Christmas tradition.

These are the lightest doughnuts I've ever tried. If you like glazed doughnuts, you'll love these! Done quickly, all 18 of them can be fried in under 20 minutes, so be sure you have a place set up to cool all of them at once before you start. Can be made in all 3 bread machines. Yield: 18 doughnuts.

Dough for 1, 1½ , or 2 lb

2 C all-purpose flour	3 T sugar
1½ T mashed potatoes*	1 tsp salt
¼ tsp nutmeg	2 T dried milk
⅝ C potato water*	2 T butter
1 egg	1½ tsp yeast
vegetable oil for deep frying	

*Or substitute 1 heaping tablespoon instant potatoes and use plain water.

TOPPING: 1 C confectioners' sugar

1. Load the bread pan of the machine with all the ingredients except the powdered sugar and oil, select the dough setting, and start it. When the beeper sounds, remove the dough to a greased bowl and chill thoroughly in the refrigerator for two hours or overnight.
2. Roll out to about a 10 × 16 inch rectangle and cut doughnut shapes with a doughnut cutter or a biscuit cutter. (If you use the biscuit cutter, just make a hole in the center with your thumb when you move them to the cookie sheet, but be sure there is a large hole, as this aids in cooking the doughnut.)
3. Place the doughnuts on a greased cookie sheet. Let them rise in a warm place for 30 minutes or until nearly doubled in bulk. If you find that the holes have closed during the rising process, just take the handle of your spatula and enlarge them.
4. Put oil at least 2 inches deep in a heavy saucepan and heat it to 375°F (191°C). Slide each doughnut into the deep fat, using a spatula that has been dipped in hot fat. Do only three or four at a time. Fry the doughnuts until brown.
6. Drain on absorbent paper; then cool on a rack. Toss with confectioners' sugar.

Variation: Glazed Doughnuts

SUGAR DOUGHNUT GLAZE

1 C confectioners' sugar	⅓ C boiling water
1 C chopped peanuts walnuts, or pecans (optional)	½ tsp vanilla, grated lemon rind, or cinnamon (optional)

1. Mix the boiling water with the sugar. If you like more flavor in your glaze, add ½ tsp vanilla, grated lemon rind, or cinnamon. Dip the warm doughnuts (see Potato Doughnut recipe) into the warm glaze.
2. If you like nuts, dip the doughnuts into finely chopped peanuts, walnuts, or pecans while the glaze is still sticky.

CHOCOLATE DOUGHNUT GLAZE

½ C semisweet chocolate pieces	¼ C water
1 T light corn syrup	

Melt the chocolate with the water over low heat, stirring constantly. Add the corn syrup. Dip the doughnuts in the glaze and set on a rack to cool.

Danish Pastries

My wife thought these were the main reason for the bread machine in the first place. The cheese ones are marvelous. This ideal-sized recipe fits all three sizes of bread machine. Yield: 12.

Dough for 1, 1½, or 2 lb

2 ½ C all-purpose flour	2 T sugar
¾ C milk	½ tsp salt
4 T butter	1½ tsp yeast

TO SPRINKLE ON THE DOUGH

1½ T sugar	½ T cinnamon
1 egg, beaten, for brushing on top, sealing edge, and filling	

CHEESE FILLING

1½ T sugar	3 oz cream cheese
1 tsp beaten egg	½ T lemon juice
¼ tsp vanilla	

FROSTING FOR DANISH PASTRY

½ C confectioners' sugar	1 T milk
⅛ tsp vanilla	

1. Load the bread pan of the machine with all the dough ingredients, set it on the dough cycle, and start it. When the dough is done, remove it to a greased bowl. Cover and let it rest in the refrigerator for an hour, or overnight.
2. Roll out the dough on a lightly floured surface into a 12 × 15 inch rectangle. Sprinkle the dough with a mixture of 1½ tablespoons of sugar and ½ teaspoon of cinnamon. Roll the dough up tightly into a 12-inch log. Seal the ends with beaten egg. Slice the log into 12 equal portions.
3. Place on greased cookie sheets, allowing space between the slices for rising. Sprinkle water on top. Let them rise at 90°F (32°C) for 20 to 30 minutes, or until nearly doubled in bulk.
4. Prepare the filling: combine the sugar with the softened cream cheese; gradually add the egg, lemon juice, and vanilla.
5. Enlarge the hole in the center of each pastry and insert the filling. Brush the Danish with the remaining beaten egg. Bake in a 360°F (183°C) oven for 15 to 20 minutes, or until golden brown.
6. Place on a rack to cool. Mix the confectioners' sugar, vanilla, and milk; drizzle from a spoon to decorate the tops of the Danish.

Variations on Danish Pastry

For people who don't like Cheese Danish, you can whip up the butterscotch recipe and fill a few of the Danish with it. Fills about 8 pastries.

BUTTERSCOTCH APPLE FILLING FOR DANISH

1 apple	1 T butter
3 T brown sugar	⅛ tsp cinnamon
2 T raisins*	1 T walnuts*
*Optional.	

Thinly slice the apple. Melt the butter in a small frying pan; add the pieces of apple, the brown sugar, and the cinnamon. Add the raisins and walnuts if you wish. Sauté until done, about 5 to 7 minutes. Cool slightly before filling the Danish.

CHERRY FILLING FOR DANISH

Fills about two dozen pastries.

1 No. 2 can (20 oz) pitted sour cherries	½ C sugar
½ tsp cinnamon (optional)	⅛ tsp salt
2 T cornstarch	

Drain the cherries, reserving the juice. Mix the sugar, cinnamon, salt and cornstarch in a saucepan. Gradually add the juice over low heat. Bring to a boil over direct heat, stirring constantly; continue cooking until clear. Add the cherries; cool slightly before using. Extra filling can be frozen for your next batch.

Holiday Breads and Rolls

Breads

Many people throughout North America and Europe just love the holidays—primarily the Christmas holidays, of course. Christmas traditionally has been the great feast. Who's going to pass up a chance to get presents and eat the way folks do around the holidays?

It was Charles Dickens, really, who put the holiday in perspective. With his marvelous powers of observation, he has left several wonderful pictures of the holiday feasts of poorest or the poor. If you read the Dickens's *A Christmas Carol,* instead of watching a film version of it, what will stick in your mind is the Cratchits' plum pudding (well, it did in mine, anyway). That was the star of the feast. But in other countries throughout Europe, it was bread, the staff of life, that was transformed for the holiday into a sweet feast. Try to imagine what it might have taken to make these loaves a hundred or so years ago, what great care was lavished on them. For those of modest means, money would have to be saved, as well as the goodies that go into the making. The loaves were one of the highlights of the holiday season. There's no reason why they can't be still.

When you read these recipes, you'll probably notice that all the loaves are pretty much alike. I've tried to retain the loaves just as they were passed on to me. Actually it was easy; the only exception was the Bohemian Christmas Loaf. Remarkably, all the recipes were in almost the exact proportions needed for the bread machine.

You can prepare the dough for all of these recipes, except for the Bohemian Christmas Loaf and the Jule Kaga, in all 3 machines, but you can't bake any of them in the 1 lb bread machine; there's no room. Any of the recipes from this section prepared in the 1 lb machine must be baked in the oven.

We'll start our tour way down south in Italy, where so much of everything started.

Panettone

Panettone–*the* Italian Christmas bread. This one I've developed on my own, and in doing so tried to capture the flavor and texture of Alamagna brand Panettone. I've come close. Ideally, you should have about an 8-inch diameter, deep-sided pan, like a spring-form pan. But you can use a regular 8-inch cake pan and build it up with a piece of aluminum foil cut to fit the circumference (remember how to calculate that? Circumference = 3.14 times the diameter), folded over and fit on the side of the pan. This recipe will fit in all 3 sizes of bread machine on the dough cycle.

Dough for 1, 1½, or 2 lb

¾ C milk	1 egg + 1 egg yolk
4 T butter	1½ T honey
2½ C all-purpose flour	2 tsp grated lemon rind
½ tsp of cardamom	1 tsp salt
¼ C raisins	¼ C candied fruit
¼ C broken walnuts or pecans	¾ C brandy to marinate
2 tsp yeast	the fruit and nuts

TOPPING: 2 T melted butter

1. Marinate the fruit and nuts in the brandy for 15 minutes.
2. Load the bread pan of the bread machine with all the ingredients except the topping, and select the dough cycle. When the dough is done, place it in a lightly greased bowl, cover the dough, and let it rest in the refrigerator for 30 minutes.
3. Lay a sheet of waxed paper on the bottom of the spring-form or 8-inch cake pan. Cut a 5- or 6-inch-wide piece of waxed paper to line the sides. Place the dough in the pan. Spray with a fine mist of water. Let it rise in a warm place for 90 minutes, or until nearly doubled in bulk.
4. Brush the Panettone with melted butter. Bake in a 350°F (177°C) oven for 35 to 40 minutes. Cool on a rack.

Variation of Panettone

When it is ready to bake, brush it with a mixture of egg yolk and a little milk or cream, sprinkle with sugar or colored sprinkles, and bake as directed.

Stollen

Now north to Germany. Excess in another way: ingredients. The Germans load their holiday bread with tasty fruits and nuts. The kneading and first rise are done on the dough cycle and the Stollen is baked in the oven in a crescent shape. Then, if you can, let it age for a day or two to ripen the flavor. You can make the dough in all 3 sizes of machine. Yield: a 1½ lb loaf.

Dough for 1, 1½, or 2 lb

⅝ C water	1 egg
1 T oil	¼ C milk
3 T butter	2¼ C all-purpose flour
2 T sugar	½ tsp salt
2 tsp yeast	

FRUIT AND NUTS

¼ C raisins	½ C candied fruits
½ tsp grated lemon peel	¼ tsp cardamom
¼ C chopped pecans	½ tsp mace

FILLING

¼ C melted butter	1 T sugar
½ tsp cinnamon	

FROSTING AND TOPPING

½ C sifted confectioners' sugar	1½ tsp milk
2 T melted butter*	¼ C slivered almonds
¼ C candied cherries	1 egg, beaten for brushing
*Reserved from the filling.	on top

1. Prepare the dough ingredients on the dough setting of your machine. When the dough is done, remove it to a bowl. Knead in the fruit, nuts, cardamom, and mace. Cover and let it rest in the refrigerator for at least 30 minutes.
2. Roll out the dough on a lightly floured surface into a 9 × 15 inch oval. Brush part of the ¼ cup of melted butter over the oval, saving what you don't use for the frosting. Sprinkle 1 tablespoon of sugar, mixed with the ¼ tsp cinnamon, over the buttered dough.
3. Keeping its length the same, fold the width of the oval in half like a big Parker House Roll (fig. a and b). Carefully lift the folded roll and move it to a lightly greased baking sheet; flatten and curve the ends slightly (fig. c).
4. Press the folded side slightly (not the open edges) to help the loaf keep its shape during rising and baking.

5. Sprinkle water on top. Set your oven to 360°F (183°C). Let the dough rise in a warm place for about an hour, or until nearly doubled in bulk.
6. Brush the top with a beaten egg.
7. Bake in a 360°F oven for 30 to 35 minutes, or until golden brown. Mix the confectioners' sugar, milk, and melted butter together to make the frosting. While the Stollen is still hot, brush it with frosting and decorate with slivered almonds and sliced candied cherries. Cool on a rack. Allow it to age for two or three days for the flavors to ripen—by putting it in a wall safe.

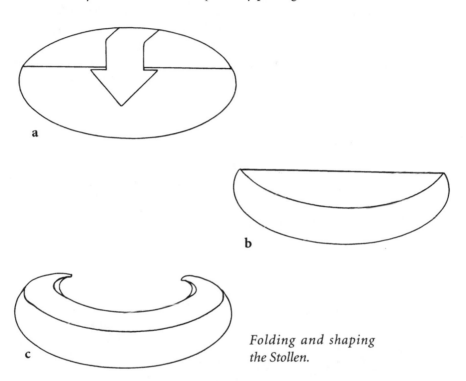

Folding and shaping the Stollen.

Swiss Christmas Loaf

Now let's go to Switzerland. While it's true enough that all these Christmas loaves are pretty much alike, this one manages to carry excess to new heights. You can put on 2½ pounds just reading the recipe, and the food police (or the Association for Terrorizing People Who Like to Eat) might raid your kitchen. But I have to tell you, I love this recipe! It is one of only two recipes I've ever taken from the original source that has worked in the bread machine as is. Okay, I made one change from the original; I added more cream to maintain the right proportions. But the finished product is . . . superlatives can't even begin to keep up. I think this is what a fruit cake was supposed to be like: soft, tender, rich, subtly tasty. One of these per season is probably enough. You can prepare the dough for this recipe on the dough cycle in all 3 sizes of bread machine. Yield: a 2-lb loaf of bread.

Dough: 1, 1½ lb or 2 lb

1 C light cream	¼ C water
3 T soft butter	1 egg
3¼ C all-purpose flour	⅓ C sugar
1 tsp salt	2 tsp yeast

FRUIT AND NUTS

¼ C raisins	¼ C chopped blanched
¼ C mixed candied fruits	almonds
2 T brandy	½ tsp cinnamon
½ tsp grated lemon peel	

1. Start by combining the light cream, ¼ cup water, and soft butter and heating them just to finger hot (100°F or 37.8°C) in a saucepan before adding them to the bread pan of your bread machine with the other dough ingredients.
2. At this point you have to decide whether you want to bake the loaf in your bread machine (you can only do this if you have a 1½ or 2 lb machine) or make the dough in the machine and bake it in your oven.
3. If you are baking in the bread machine, add the fruit and nuts when the fruit beeper goes off (if you have a fruit beeper), or 10 to 15 minutes after the machine has been kneading the dough.
4. If you are doing only the dough cycle in the machine, you have more latitude. You can either knead the fruit and nuts in and make a regular or braided loaf, or roll the dough out, spread the fruit and nuts on it, and roll it up. Bake in a 360°F (183°C) oven for 35 or 40 minutes.

Bohemian Christmas Loaf

The ingredients will only fit in the 1½ pound machine and 2 lb machine on the dough cycle. They won't fit in the 1 lb machine at all. Yield: a 2-lb loaf.

Dough (1½ or 2 lb)

1 C milk*	¼ C water*
3 T soft butter*	⅓ C sugar*
2 tsp salt*	½ tsp grated lemon peel*
½ tsp mace (or nutmeg)*	2 eggs
4½ C all-purpose flour	2½ tsp yeast

FRUIT, NUTS, AND SPICES

½ tsp cinnamon	½ C chopped blanched almonds or almond paste
½ C raisins	1 T brandy

1. Put the first seven dough ingredients (with asterisks) in a saucepan and heat to about 100°F to 110°F (38 to 43°C). Then put them in the bread pan before the rest of the dough ingredients.
2. Now add the next three ingredients: eggs, flour, and yeast.
3. At this point, decide whether you want to bake the loaf in your bread machine or in the oven. If you are going to bake it in the bread machine, add the fruit, nuts, and spices when the fruit beeper goes off (if you have one), about 10 to 15 minutes after the machine has been kneading the dough. If you are baking the loaf in the oven, and just preparing the dough on the dough cycle, you have more latitude; you can either knead the fruit and nuts into the dough and make a regular or braided loaf, or roll the dough out, spread the fruit and nuts on it, and roll it up as a log. The original recipe (heaven knows how old it is) suggests the option of spreading almond paste on the dough and rolling it up into a loaf. It also called for braiding three strips of dough and then adding a fourth braid down the center. Bake at 350°F (177°C).

Danish Holiday Twist Loaf

Wonderfully easy, rich, and elegant, a tasty Christmas morning treat. I have even made this when there is no holiday to celebrate. Serve it with coffee, of course. Yield: 1¼ lb (small) or 2 lb loaf (large).

Small Dough (1 or 1½ lb)	Large Dough (1½ or 2 lb)
1 C milk	1¼ C milk
1 egg	1 egg
6 T soft butter	½ C (4 oz) soft butter
3 C all-purpose flour	4 C all-purpose flour
⅓ C sugar	½ C sugar
½ tsp salt	½ rounded tsp salt
1 tsp ground cardamom	1½ tsp ground cardamom
1 tsp yeast	1½ tsp yeast

GLAZE: 1 egg, beaten with ½ tsp salt

TOPPING: ½ C shredded almonds

1. Put all the dough ingredients in the bread machine. Set it to the dough setting, and start it.
2. Remove the dough from the bread pan when it is done. Press all of the air out of the dough. Let it rest for a few minutes; then divide the dough into three equal portions. Roll and stretch them into long ropes, and braid them loosely, to form a plait.
3. Place the plait on a greased cookie sheet, tuck the ends under, and let it rise for 30 minutes in a warm place.
4. With the oven at 375°F (191°C), beat the egg and salt together for the glaze and brush the loaf with it. Sprinkle with the almonds.
5. Bake for 30 or 35 minutes. Let it cool; then slice it and eat it with butter.

Jule Kaga

Quite a bit like the Swiss loaf, but a shade less rich—it uses milk instead of cream, and less of it, and no eggs. It too uses that wonderful cardamom. This loaf will be too big for a 1-lb machine, even on the dough cycle. Yields a 2-lb loaf of bread.

Dough for 1½ or 2 lb

¾ C milk	½ C water
stick (4 oz) soft butter	4¼ C all-purpose flour
½ C sugar	1 tsp cardamom
1 tsp salt	2 tsp yeast

FRUIT AND NUTS

¼ C chopped blanched almonds	½ C raisins
¼ C mixed candied cherries	¼ C chopped citron

1. Start by combining the milk, water, and butter, and heat them in a saucepan to about 100°F (38°C) before adding them to the bread pan of the bread machine.
2. Add the rest of the dough ingredients, and set the machine to the dough cycle. You could add everything in the Fruit and Nuts ingredients when the fruit beeper goes off (or 10 to 15 minutes after the machine has been kneading the dough). Or you could add the fruit and nuts later when you're kneading the bread by hand.
3. When the beeper sounds, remove the dough to a bowl and let it rest for 30 minutes in the refrigerator.
4. Turn out onto a lightly floured surface and knead lightly, adding in the fruit and nuts if you didn't add them earlier.
5. Shape the loaf in a log, let it rise about 45 minutes, and bake in a 350°F (177°C) oven for about 40 to 45 minutes. Coat it while warm with a frosting (see frosting for Hot Cross Buns).

English Christmas Bread

The following is the least rich of all the holiday loaves, and maybe the tastiest. The medium recipe will fit in all 3 machines on the dough cycle; the large recipe will fit in the 1½ or 2 lb bread machine. Yield: 1½ lb (medium) or 2+ lb (large) loaf.

Medium Dough (all 3 sizes)	Large Dough (1½ or 2 lb)
¾ C milk	1 C milk
⅓ C water	½ C water
2 T soft butter	3 T soft butter
3 C all-purpose flour	4¼ C all-purpose flour
⅓ C sugar	½ C sugar
½ tsp cinnamon	¾ tsp cinnamon
¼ tsp nutmeg	½ tsp nutmeg
1 tsp salt	1½ tsp salt
2 tsp yeast	2½ tsp yeast
FRUIT	**FRUIT**
½ C raisins	¾ C raisins
¼ C chopped citron	⅓ C chopped citron

TOPPING: 1 T confectioners' sugar

1. In the bread machine, add the dough ingredients in order and set the machine to the dough cycle. You can add the fruit when the fruit beeper goes off or about 10 to 15 minutes after the machine has been kneading the dough. Or you can knead the fruit in by hand after you take the dough from the bread machine.
2. Let the dough rest in the refrigerator for 30 minutes in a greased bowl after it has been removed from the bread machine.
3. Knead the dough lightly for 2 minutes, adding the fruit if you didn't do so before. Shape the loaf and let it rise for 30 minutes in a warm place on a greased cookie sheet.
4. Bake in the oven at 350°F (177°C) until golden brown, or about 35 to 45 minutes.
5. Coat it after baking, while still hot, with a clear glaze by sprinkling confectioners' sugar on it.

Rolls

Hot Cross Buns

These lovely Lenten treats were served on Sundays during Lent. They are quint-essentially English, and sometimes are known as spring rolls. They are not terribly sweet. This is it, the one item that even the French yield to the English. By the way, if you don't have cardamom, you can substitute nutmeg. But for heaven's sake just go ahead and get some cardamom! This recipe fits in all 3 sizes of bread machine on the dough cycle. Yield: 9.

Dough for 1, 1½, or 2 lb

2½ C all-purpose flour	¾ C water
¼ C milk	½ tsp salt
1 egg	¼ tsp cinnamon
2 T butter	½ tsp cardamom
1 T sugar	1 tsp yeast

FRUIT (all sizes)

½ C raisins (plumped)*	⅓ C candied citrus rind

*See page 46 for instructions for plumping raisins.

TOPPING: One egg, beaten with 2 T water (egg wash).

1. Load the bread pan of the bread machine with the dough ingredients, select the dough setting, and start the machine.
2. When the beeper sounds, remove the dough to a lightly greased bowl. Cover. let the dough rest in the refrigerator for 30 minutes or, even better, overnight.
3. Then, on a floured surface, knead in the raisins and candied citrus rind.
4. Divide the dough into 9 equal pieces. Place each piece, not touching the others, in a 10-inch-square heat-resistant (Pyrex) baking dish (if you have it), in three rows of three, or otherwise in a similar size metal pan.
5. Let the buns rise in a warm place, covered with plastic wrap, for 45 minutes, or until they are just touching.
6. Coat the tops with the egg wash and bake for 20 to 25 minutes in a 350°F (177°C) oven, until they are beautifully browned. Remove from the pan and set on a cooling rack.
7. When they are cooled somewhat (they are, after all, *hot* cross buns) make lines down the middle of each bun with the frosting. Then turn the pan a quarter turn and make lines crossing the first lines on each one. Each bun should now have a cross on it—hence the name.

VANILLA FROSTING FOR HOT CROSS BUNS

½ C confectioners' sugar   1¼ tsp milk

¼ tsp vanilla extract

Combine the ingredients and stir. It may seem that there is not enough milk in the recipe, but the sugar will dissolve it. The thicker the frosting is, the easier it will set up.

Saffransbröd, or Christmas Saffron Buns

This is a Scandinavian treat with a really interesting flavor, quite similar to the Swedish Christmas loaf. This recipe makes 18 to 20 buns—depending on the designs you pick. It may be used in all 3 sizes of bread machine on the dough cycle.

Dough for 1, 1½, and 2 lb

pinch of saffron   ¼ C boiling water

1 C milk   3 T butter

1 egg   ½ C sugar

½ tsp salt   3¼ C flour

1½ tsp yeast

a few oz of raisins for decorating

GLAZE: 1 egg beaten with ½ tsp salt

1. Soak a pinch of saffron in ¼ cup boiling water for a half-hour. Put the saffron water into the bread pan first; then add the milk and butter to the warm mixture, so the butter will melt; then add the egg. Then add the sugar, salt, flour, and yeast. Select the dough cycle.
2. When the dough is done, remove it to a floured surface. Knead all the air out and let rest for 10 minutes.
3. Take a small handful of dough and roll it into a rope; then shape it into one or more of the shapes shown. Continue to make as many as you wish.
4. Put raisins in the inner curls of the dough, as shown. Place the dough twists on a greased baking sheet. Coat them with the egg glaze and bake them in a 400°F (205°C) oven for 15 minutes, or until golden. Cool on a wire rack.

Note: This recipe can also be made as a loaf or braid. Makes a 1½ lb bread.

Some traditional shapes for Saffransbröd.

Meals from the Bread Machine

For most of the Western world, bread is truly the basic food, the staff of life, and consequently it is part and parcel of a fascinating variety of meals. Many are made with or from bread dough. Several of the bread recipes in this book are meals in themselves—just add a salad and perhaps onion soup. Let's begin with breakfast.

Hawaiian or Breakfast Pizza

The only way to start the day for people who prefer to eat nothing but pizza. Yield: regular, 12-inch pizza; large, 15-inch pizza. Prepare on the dough cycle. Both recipes will fit in all 3 machines.

Regular Dough (1, 1½ or 2 lb)	**Large Dough** (1, 1½ or 2 lb)
¼ C milk	¼ C milk
⅝ C water	1 C water
2¼ C flour	3 C flour
2 T sugar	3 T sugar
1½ T butter	2 T butter
1 tsp salt	1 rounded tsp salt
1½ tsp yeast	2 tsp yeast

TOPPING (both sizes)

½ stick (2 oz) butter

1 C brown sugar

16 oz can crushed pineapple, drained

¼ C pineapple juice, reserved from can

1. Load the dough ingredients into your bread machine, select the dough cycle, and start the machine. When the dough is done, remove it to a greased bowl. Cover it and let the dough rest in the refrigerator for 30 minutes or overnight.
2. Divide the dough into two or three balls, or size to suit your pizza pans. Roll each ball into a flat circle, flattening and stretching it from the center out until it's large enough to fill the pizza pans.
3. Grease the pizza pans with butter or margarine. Place the pizza dough on the pans, and prick surface all over with a fork.

4. To prepare the topping: Melt the butter in a saucepan. Stir in the brown sugar and the ¼ cup of pineapple juice. Cook, stirring, over a low flame, until thickened. Spread the brown sugar sauce on each pizza; then top it with the crushed pineapple.
5. Bake in a 400°F (205°C) oven for 10 minutes, covered with a sheet of aluminum foil, and then 5 to 7 minutes uncovered. Serve hot.

Frog Dogs

Almost a meal, Frog Dogs are probably the quickest, easiest recipe, and one that's always a crowd-pleaser with our kids. We serve them with French fries and cole slaw to round out the meal. Yield: regular, 6 large or 8 small. Banquet size: 12 to 20. The regular batch fits in all 3 machines on the dough cycle. The banquet size batch fits in the 1½ or 2 lb machine.

Regular Dough (1, 1½ or 2 lb)	Banquet Size (1 or 1½ lb)
⅞ C water	1¼ C water
2¼ C flour	4 C flour
1 tsp lard or olive oil	2 tsp lard or olive oil
1 tsp salt	2 tsp salt
1 tsp yeast	1½ tsp yeast
ACCOMPANIMENTS	**ACCOMPANIMENTS**
cole slaw	cole slaw
6 or 8 frankfurters	12 to 20 frankfurters
mustard	mustard
onions	onions
sliced cheese (optional)	sliced cheese (optional)

1. Load the dough ingredients into your bread machine in the order it suggests and set it for the dough cycle. When the dough is ready, move it from the bread machine onto a floured surface, press all the air out of the dough, and let it rest for 10 minutes.
2. After the dough has rested, divide it into the number of pieces sufficent for your frankfurters. Flatten each piece to ¼ inch, and shape it into a thin oval.
3. Place a frankfurter on the dough and fold the dough over it, covering it. (By the way, you can wrap the frankfurter in cheese first, maybe even spread on some mustard or add onions–think about it.) Place the frog dog in a warm place to rise for about 10 to 15 minutes. Bake at 350°F (177°C) for 15 to 20 minutes, or until brown.

Pizza

For more serious meals, ones that even have food value, first and foremost is pizza. I have in my library a marvelous book on Italian cooking. It surveys the various regions of Italy and describes how they cook. There are at least a half-dozen different recipes for pizza. What does this tell you? Right! Pizzas are the way good Italian mothers got rid of their leftovers—the Italian equivalent of the American casserole, on a bread crust. What we present here barely scratches the surface of the varieties of this marvelous thing to eat. Probably after making it two or three times, yours will surpass any you can have delivered—at a third the cost.

For a change, instead of making large pizzas, you can make individual pizzas and top each to taste, so that everyone has the topping he wants and is happy. Bake them on a cookie sheet.

Pizza with Tomato Sauce

This recipe will fit in all 3 machines on the dough cycle. Yield: regular size, 12-inch pizza; large, 15-inch pizza.

Regular Dough (1, 1½ or 2 lb)	Large Dough (1, 1½ or 2 lb)
2¼ C flour	3 C flour
⅞ C water	1⅛ C water
1 tsp salt	1½ tsp salt
1 T olive oil	1½ T olive oil
1 tsp yeast	1½ tsp yeast

For both: cornmeal or olive oil for the pizza pans

TOPPING (for both sizes)

4 oz grated Parmesan cheese

dried oregano

about 4 oz per pizza of pepperoni, sausage, bacon, anchovies, mushrooms, or similar topping

½ pound or more shredded mozzarella cheese for the regular pizza and ¾ lb to 1 lb for the large

TOMATO SAUCE FOR PIZZA (both sizes)

Use your own favorite sauce or the quick and simple tasty one given here. (Of course, you can just use your leftover spaghetti sauce or, in summertime, just slice several fresh tomatoes and lay on a basil leaf and a clove of garlic, instead of sauce. If you use the fresh tomatoes, bake the crust for 15 minutes first. Then add the tomatoes, basil, and garlic, and bake for 5 minutes more.

1 or 2 (or 3 or 4) cloves garlic	1 tsp dried basil (or 1 T fresh)
½ tsp dried oregano (or 1 tsp fresh)	3 T tomato paste
¼ C water	1 T olive oil
salt and pepper to taste	

Prepare the sauce as follows: lightly sauté the garlic, basil and oregano to fragrance. Add the tomato paste, olive oil, salt, pepper, and water. Stir gently to a low simmer until thickened.

1. To make the pizza, load the dough ingredients into your bread machine in the order suggested in its instructions, and set it for the dough cycle.
2. When the beeper sounds, remove the dough, let it rest for a few minutes and proceed, or put it in a lightly oiled bowl, cover, and refrigerate until you need it. Make your sauce if you haven't already done so.
3. Divide the dough into one, two, or three balls, depending on the size of your pizza pans.
4. Roll each ball into a flat circle, flattening and stretching it from the center out until it is large enough to fill the pizza pan. Let it rest.
5. Now spread olive oil on the pizza pans or sprinkle each with a tablespoon of cornmeal. Place the pizza dough in the pan, and stretch it until it fits. Prick the surface all over with a fork. Give it a good spreading of Parmesan cheese. Spread with pizza sauce to taste.
6. Top with mozzarella cheese; add pepperoni (or mushrooms, anchovies, sautéed green peppers, onions, fresh tomato slices, olives, sprigs of basil topped with slices of garlic, etc.) and sprinkle generously with oregano.
7. Bake in a 450°F (232°C) oven for 15 minutes, or until done.

White Pizza

For the dough, use the ingredients from Pizza with Tomato Sauce.

TOPPINGS (both sizes)

½ medium onion, chopped

1 C or more grated mozzarella

olives, black or kalamata*

anchovies*

1 T finely chopped parsley

2 T olive oil

3 cloves garlic, minced

1 C or more ricotta cheese

2 T Parmesan and Romano cheese

*Optional.

This is a variation of the Pizza with Tomato Sauce recipe. Use the dough recipe for Pizza with Tomato Sauce, through Step 4. Substitute the toppings given here.

5. After the pizza dough is on the sheet or pans, spread the top generously with good olive oil; then use this recipe our wonderful daughter Kirsten came up with (the girl's a great cook).
6. Sauté the onions and garlic in olive oil until transparent; then mix in about a cup of ricotta cheese (it depends how big your crust is and how much you like it), add a couple of tablespoons of grated Parmesan and Romano and a tablespoon of finely chopped parsley. Spread this on the crust and top with lots of mozzarella and, depending on how gutsy you are, you can dot the tops with black or kalamata olives and anchovies. Serve with a lively white wine, don't get too close to people, and think twice before kissing.

Stromboli

Basically a rolled pizza; one of countless varieties you can make. As for the origins of the pizza, it was a way to hide a lot of good but inedible-looking larder gleanings. With kids and other fussy eaters, a good rule of thumb is: if they can't see what it is, they can't refuse to eat it.

The primary difference between Stromboli the way we like it and the Tuscan Tailgate Loaf is that Stromboli uses pizza dough and is less portable—it can be awfully messy. Yield: Regular, 8 × 12 inch Stromboli; large, 11 × 14 inch Stromboli.

For the dough, use the regular or large dough ingredients list from Pizza with Tomato Sauce.

STROMBOLI FILLING (for either size of pizza)

½ lb grated mozzarella cheese

1 medium onion and 1 clove garlic, both chopped, sautéed together

1 cup of nutritious meat scraps (cappiciola, prosciutto, pepperoni, ham, chicken, veal, etc.)

leftover broccoli florets, olives, etc.

½ C tomato (spaghetti) sauce

1. Load the dough ingredients into your bread machine in the order suggested in its instructions and set it for the dough cycle.
2. When the beeper sounds, remove the dough and let it rest for a few minutes and proceed, or put it in a lightly oiled bowl, cover, and refrigerate until you need it.
3. Set the oven to 400°F (205°C). Roll out the dough into a ¼-inch-thick oblong. Spread the tomato sauce on half the dough (lengthwise) and heap on all the other filling ingredients.
4. Fold the dough over on itself, seal, and bake for 25 minutes in a 400°F oven. Serve with wine and by candlelight—candlelight hides a multitude of sins.

Tuscan Tailgate Loaf

This meal is so named because the first time my wife made it was for a tailgate party. It is served warm; she made it in the morning and we kept the loaf (well wrapped in aluminum foil) inside the engine compartment of our Fiat. Since we had been driving for 5 hours, it was was nice and hot! This recipe will fit in all 3 bread machines on the dough cycle. Yield: one 10 × 16 inch loaf.

Dough for 1, 1½ or 2 lb

2½ C all-purpose flour	1 C water
1 tsp salt	3 T olive oil
1 T sugar	½ C grated cheddar cheese
2 tsp yeast	

FILLING

1 lb Italian sausage*	1 small chopped onion
1 C grated provolone or mozzarella cheese	2 T tomato sauce**

*See also the Chorizo recipe on the next page.
**Optional.

TOPPING: one egg, beaten

1. Load the dough ingredients into your bread machine in the order suggested in its instructions; set it on the dough cycle.
2. Prepare the filling: brown the sausage and onion together, drain off the fat, and cool.
3. When the beeper sounds, remove the dough to a bowl. Cover. Let the dough rest in the refrigerator for 30 minutes.
4. Roll out the dough on a lightly floured surface into a 10 × 16 inch rectangle. Sprinkle half of the dough with half of the cheese. Spread the rest of the filling over the dough; then sprinkle the rest of the cheese on the filling.
5. Starting at one end, loosen the dough so that it can be lifted.
6. Now carefully fold the dough in half lengthwise, forming a 5 × 16 inch log. Brush the edges with beaten egg and seal. Set the oven to 360°F (183°C).
7. Place on a greased baking pan. Sprinkle the top with water. Let it rise at 90°F (32°C) for 20 to 30 minutes, or until nearly doubled in bulk.
8. Brush top with a beaten egg. Bake in a 360° F oven for 30 minutes, or until golden brown. Serve hot or cold.

Variations of Tuscan Tailgate Loaf

The sausage and onion can be replaced with or have the following added to them: mushrooms, peppers, pepperoni and/or anything else you would normally like in Stromboli or on Pizza.

Chorizo

Italian sausage is what my wife used first in the Tuscan Tailgate Loaf. Since then, she has taken to using a Spanish sausage called *chorizo*. Many independent or regional grocery stores make their own sausage. Sausage, real sausage, is nothing more than chopped pork with coarse salt and coarsely ground black pepper. It is best to add the herbs (sage, rosemary, etc.) shortly before cooking. Here is my wife's recipe for Chorizo. Yield: 1 to 1½ lbs.

1 to 1½ lbs ground pork	1½ tsp coarse salt
1½ tsp paprika	1 tsp oregano
1 tsp red pepper	1 clove garlic, chopped
1½ T vinegar	1½ T water
¼ tsp coarse ground black pepper	

1. Mix all the ingredients thoroughly. Let them sit for several hours to blend the flavors better.
2. Fry in a skillet until cooked, and use in Tuscan Tailgate Loaf.

APPENDIXES

About Bread Machines

Let's talk about bread machines. What a wonderful gadget is the bread machine! It has to rank with the sewing machine, and maybe the espresso machine, as among the most worthwhile inventions of the past 200 years. In fact, I wrote to the Nobel Prize committee to express my opinion that the inventor deserved consideration for a prize. It wasn't a joke or a publicity shtick. I just think about bread machines and their potential for good—providing good, nutritious, healthy bread, inexpensively, to millions of people, and with virtually no work. I mean, if some theorist on economics that no one can understand can warrant a Nobel Prize, then why not the inventor of the wonderful bread machine?

It's a reasonable presumption that having gone this far in the book, you either have a bread machine or are fairly serious about getting one. I've noticed many people start with one of the less expensive bread machines; then, finding out how marvelous they are, they go on to buy a better, or more expensive machine, anyway. Then they give the first one to the kids. But if you're one of those who still doesn't have a bread machine, and you want an "expert" opinion before spending money on a machine, allow me.

We bought our first bread machine, a Panasonic, back in February of 1991. Then there were only about 5 different machines on the market. Since then maybe a dozen new machines have appeared, and a few have disappeared. At this writing, they sell about 3 million each year in the US alone.

All the prices have come down and the quality has improved (it was pretty good to start with). The sizes have increased from the handy little 1-pound loaf machines, up to the 2 pounders that are now common. By the time you read this, there will be machines capable of making 3-pound loaves of bread. That's one loaf of bread! (I remember when we were making lunches for half a dozen kids every morning. A 3-pound loaf would have been great.) But the 1½ or 2 pounders are the most common and do nicely for even a fairly large family.

All the bread machines make a pretty good loaf of bread. They all look and work pretty much the same. Nice-looking gadgets they are, which take up about a square foot, more or less, of counter space, stand a little over a foot high, and all are more or less the same color. They all have a removable bread pan, in which is inserted a removable kneading paddle. They all come with a cheap, opaque plastic measuring cup that is almost impossible to read and is of dubious accuracy. They all have owner's manuals of various degrees of readability, and some have separate recipe booklets. The more expensive ones usually include a package of bread mix and yeast samples. Most of the machines have little windows in the top to peek in and see what's happening. They all have control panels with flat buttons, and LED screens that, depending on the machine, will tell you what's going on and what time it is and when the bread is going to be done. And I've even heard of one that speaks!

These machines range in price. From the cheapest to the most expensive, if you use your machine regularly for all your baking—breads, dinner rolls, sweet rolls, whatever—it can save you enough money to pay for itself in a reasonable length of time, while offering a dramatic improvement in quality, not to mention nutritional value, over what you've been used to eating as bread.

If parents would use the machine to supply most of their kids' treats and then wean the kids off soft drinks (just give them iced tea or lemonade instead), people would spend far less on health care. This helps dieters, too. If you fill up on bread, which is good for you, you aren't hungry for junk that isn't.

Back to the machines: I've tested my recipes in about a dozen machines. All the bread machines make a good loaf of bread; several make fine loaves. I did have one that I would call a bad machine; by that I mean a poorly thought out machine—rather expensive, with an instruction book that was hard to read and harder to figure out. But even it made a decent, if too large, loaf of bread.

Some machines also make cakes (small, square, funny-looking ones, to be sure) and jams; some mix cookie dough and even pasta; and one, one very good one I might add, even makes butter! I have only heard of one that didn't have a dough cycle. (Be sure to get one that does have a dough cycle.) Some machines have beepers which tell you when to add raisins, fruit, and nuts; some beep to tell you to dress up the crust. Some come with a special kneader paddle that won't chew up raisins in the raisin bread. Many have a whole wheat and/or a rye cycle; one makes more than one loaf at a time; some make loaves that look rather traditional, some are round, and some tall.

So, then, what is the next machine you're going to buy? You could read some reviews of bread machines in *Consumer Reports*. Or you can take my advice. Let's presume that you started with an inexpensive machine, an "off brand," one that no one has heard of, and you want to move up. If you stick with the brand names and pay in the moderate price range, you're probably going to get something that will last a good 5 years, and maybe longer.

This doesn't mean that it will be perfect for you or that it will be trouble-free. Things change, especially with bread machines. The competition is stiff, and manufacturers are constantly updating, improving, doing their best to win your money. Most, if not all, of the machines are good. There are maybe three or four that I would have to call superior. But ultimately, it is the recipes that make the biggest difference—hence this book. Before you rush out to buy your first machine, or another one, read the next chapter, Alternate Bread Machines.

Alternate Bread Machines

While I was signing books and demonstrating bread machines in Pittsburgh, I met a lady who said she loved my recipes. I asked her what kind of bread machine she had. She replied that she made her bread in a food processor.

"You make bread in a food processor?" I asked, incredulously.

"Sure. Been doing it for years. It's faster, and I have more control over everything."

That conversation kind of got filed away in the back of my mind and I thought no more about it, until sometime later. I was watching a Julia Child cooking video. In it, the grand lady of cooking demonstrated how to make French bread using a food processor. "Hmmmm, there it is again," thought I, rather loudly, remembering the lady in Pittsburgh.

That reminded me of Judith Olney's wonderful bread book, and her mentioning one of her cohorts insisting on using his mixer to prepare bread dough. I've since talked to others who use mixers regularly.

Well, it finally dawned on me that the wonderful little bread machines aren't the only bread-making machines after all. There are others, and while you can't exactly "make bread in them," you can make bread using them. And, as the good lady said, it's faster, and you can have more control over everything.

Now then, let's say you have one of those less-expensive bread machines. You've found it to be a marvelous gadget, and now you're seriously considering buying a better or more expensive and fancier bread machine.

Remember, I said that all the bread machines make a pretty good loaf of bread. I also mentioned that many people, after several months of baking bread in their machine, try rolls and pizza dough using the dough cycle. Then, invariably, they start finishing the bread dough by hand and baking it in their oven. The truth is, while the machines are wonderful, handy, simple, easy, et cetera, there is still no substitute for hand-finished bread. What follows then is directed to those people interested in a "newer" and "better" machine, and those mentioned above (the hand finishers).

Suppose, instead of buying another, better bread machine, which might cost you quite a bit, you were to consider buying a food processor. Food processors which have the power to handle bread dough are in the same price range. And a mixer with enough power to handle bread dough is also. Would one of these machines prove as handy in making bread as a less expensive bread machine? Could they even beat the marvelous bread machine? Well, I've tested several of them, and I can tell you, they get pretty close. Admittedly, they are not the "dump in the ingredients and three hours later you've got a loaf of bread" kind of easy, but they do simplify making bread, and they offer many other uses into the bargain. (You can't slice onions or tomatoes in your bread machine.) And in some of the larger mixers you can make dough for the equivalent of three large loaves (10 cups of white flour), or a pizza the size of Rhode Island, or use six cups of whole wheat flour at one time.

I've tested several of the good machines, and I can recommend them as realistic alternatives. They aren't load-and-bake machines, but they reduce the amount of time involved in making dough to a total of about 10 minutes.

The other day we were going to have pizza, so I did the following in a food processor:

1. Grated about ½ pound of Parmesan cheese and put it in the shaker. That took a minute or two. Then, without cleaning the bowl of the food processor, I

2. Shredded ½ pound of mozzarella (for the top of the pizza) and put it in a separate bowl for later. That took another minute or two. Then, again without cleaning the food processor bowl, I

3. Put the steel blade in the machine and took 4 sun-dried tomatoes and about ¼ pound of pepperoni, put them in the same bowl I had been using, and chopped both together until they were small chunks. I set them aside in a bowl until I

4. Put the plastic dough blade in the machine and proceeded, again using the same bowl, now with a bunch of nice flavors in it, to make the dough as I will show you in a moment, adding a tablespoon of Italian seasoning.

5. When I was through kneading the dough for the last time (it takes about one minute), I dumped in the tomatoes and pepperoni, gave it a 5-second run to mix these goodies in, and then let the dough rise for about an hour.

When I was finished and the dough was ready to be made into pizza crust, I put all the parts from the processor in the dishwasher. For those of you who consider clean-up time in your recipes, think about that!

Let's look at food processors and mixers and see if they're for you. First, and this is very important, you have to choose a machine powerful enough to handle bread dough. There are several mixers or processors with the guts to make dough. They cost about what you pay for a really good bread machine.

Remember that you must bake the bread, rolls, whatever, in your oven, not in the machines. On the other hand, both the processors and the mixers do the other tasks for which they are justifiably famous: slicing, chopping, dicing, grinding, mixing, and whipping. With some, mixers, you can buy a grain mill attachment so you can actually mill your own flour. And let me tell you, there is a difference in taste between freshly ground flour and the packaged stuff.

I've been working with these machines for quite a while and have demonstrated, to myself at least, that depending upon how much you cook, how much you like to cook, and to what degree you insist upon preparing your own food your own way, these machines are a reasonable alternative to the bread machine. They may not be quite as handy, but are far more versatile.

The food processors and the mixers that are capable of making bread dough give recipes for it. But these recipes do seem a bit complicated. For instance, on both types of machines, the recipes tell you to remove the dough, put it in a greased bowl, and let it rise in a warm place. Why bother taking the dough out of the working bowl to let it rise? Just cover the bowl if you are using the mixer. If you're using the processor, it's already covered.

The manufacturers of both types of machines suggest proofing the yeast before adding it. Proofing, or proving, means dissolving the yeast in a little warm water with a bit of sugar in it and waiting 5 or 10 minutes to see if the yeast starts to grow. With the new quick or rapid rise active dry yeasts, modern packaging and all, this is a waste of time, a carryover from the days of yeast cakes. Nevertheless, dissolving the yeast with a pinch of sugar in warm to hot water for a few minutes before adding it does seem to make the yeast work a bit better.

You can use all my recipes in either a mixer or a food processor. There are only three things that must be done a little differently in these machines, as opposed to the bread machine:

1. You activate the yeast before adding it. You start the whole operation with fairly warm water, about 110°F (43°C). Measure ¼ to ⅓ of a cup of warm water into your measuring cup. Add the correct amount of yeast for the recipe and a pinch of sugar. Stir this up, set it aside, and let it begin to "work" for a few minutes. While the yeast is working, you measure the dry ingredients into the work bowl of your food processor or mixer.

Although you can put all the dry ingredients, including the yeast, in the bowl at one time, just as you do in a regular bread machine, I've found you get a better dough by activating the yeast first. This probably has to do with the fact that in both the processor and the mixer, you are not spending much time working the dough. Bread machines work the dough for sometimes a half-hour or more. These alternate machines work the dough for only a few minutes; only a minute or so in the processor, and only 2 or 3 minutes in the mixers. But they work the dough very intensely and vigorously. (The folks at KitchenAid, for instance, have calculated that 2 or 3 minutes in one of their mixers is the equivalent of 10 of so of good old human muscle power.)

2. The amount of liquid used in the recipes must be reduced when you use a food processor or mixer. You reduce it about 10%. For instance, if the recipe calls for 1⅛ cups of water, reduce it to 1 cup.

3. Mix all the dry ingredients and the shortening first, before you add the liquid ingredients. Add the fruit and nuts last, if you're making fruit bread, as you would when working with a bread machine.

Now let's run through an actual recipe. Here's how you make the most basic of breads, Basic French Bread, in the food processor.

Basic French Bread in the Food Processor

Yield: two 16-inch baguettes.

1 C water	pinch of sugar	1½ tsp yeast
3 C flour	2 tsp salt	1 tsp olive oil

1. Use the plastic dough blade in the working bowl of the food processor. Start by putting ⅓ C of warm water (comfortably hot to the touch, which is about 110°F or 43°C) into your measuring cup, and add a pinch of sugar and the yeast. Stir it well and set it aside for a few minutes.
2. Put your flour, salt, and olive oil in the working bowl of the processor. Run it for 10 seconds to mix thoroughly.
3. When the yeast water is kind of foamy, or the yeast at least appears to be completely dissolved, start the machine and gradually add the yeast water. When it is all in the machine, stop it.
4. Now, add ⅔ cup of warm water to the same cup you had the yeast in (kind of washing the remains out). Start the machine again and slowly add this water to the dry ingredients. When you've added it all, continue to run the machine another 5 seconds. Stop it.
5. Let this mixture rest for at least 10 minutes. What's happening now is that the flour is absorbing the liquid completely.
6. After this rest period, start the machine again and run it for about 30 seconds. Stop the machine and use a spatula to scrape the wall of the bowl. Start the machine again. What you want to do is form a dough ball. After another 20 to 30 seconds, stop the machine. If you have to, open it up and help form the dough ball a bit by hand. Then put the top back on the machine again and let the dough rise in the work bowl for about an hour.
7. When that hour or so is up, use the pulse function to "knock" or "punch" the air out of the dough with two or three 2-second pulses.
8. Remove the dough to a floured surface, finish pushing the air out of it by hand, and let it rest for 5 or 10 minutes. That's it. Now you can make a baguette, or rolls, pizza dough—you name it—shaping and letting your dough rise according to the recipe and baking as directed in the oven.

I like the speed of the processors, and the fact that you can do some amazing cooking with them. And I like the fact that you can make three loaves of white bread at one time using one of the big mixers.

After reviewing the above, the question remains whether or not one of these alternate machines is worth your considering. You will simply have to answer that yourself. For ease alone, and pretty good quality too, you can't beat a bread machine. For speed and versatility, it's the processor. For general all-around use, including lots of cookie dough, saith my wife, it may be the mixer. But all in all, if you have the money and the space, I say buy all three.

Tasty Dishes
from Leftover Bread

Of course, you can always feed your leftover bread to the ducks. Then what do you have? That's right: fat ducks. Here are some delicious alternatives.

French Toast

There are as many recipes for French toast as there are Frenchmen, or better yet, Frenchwomen. Although French toast is a simple expedient devised to get rid of stale bread, it is so good that many are tempted to use fresh bread. This is unwise. Stale bread, or at least bread that is a day or two old, is much better.

In my roughly 50 years of making French toast, I have actually read recipes for it. They range from the minimalist extremes of the brilliant John Thorne to the other end of the spectrum, a recipe which I recall from the halcyon days of my youth, 35 years or so ago. I'm not sure exactly where I read it. Let's call it

French Toast Extreme for the Masses*

Makes 24 slices of French toast.

1 dozen eggs	1 T sugar
1 tsp vanilla	1 can evaporated milk
1 tsp salt	1 tsp cinnamon
24 bread slices	bacon fat for frying

*in the absence of cake.

Beat the eggs until thoroughly mixed; then add the sugar and vanilla. Beat again, then add the evaporated milk, salt, and cinnamon, continuing to beat. Dip the bread slices into this mixture and cook on a griddle in bacon fat.

Golden Mean French Toast

Here is the recipe I've settled on, the one we use most often. One basic portion should feed two people, with maybe six slices of bread machine bread. (Remember that bread machine bread is richer and more filling than bread sold in stores.)

1 egg, beaten, combined with ¾ C milk	1 pinch of salt
1 dash of vanilla, or anise, Triple Sec, etc.	1 tsp sugar
2 T margarine and 2 T butter	6 slices of stale bread

1. Add the salt, sugar, and vanilla or liqueur to the milk and eggs. Beat thoroughly. Dip the bread into the mixture.
2. Put the butter and margarine together on the skillet, and when they are nicely melted and starting to bubble, lay the pieces of dipped bread on and cook until golden.

For the past 15 years we have made our own syrup. It takes 5 minutes, is ridiculously easy, and once you make your syrup, you will probably never buy store-bought syrup again. We started making our own simple syrup after a friend gave us a gallon of Vermont maple syrup. We loved it. When we ran out of the Vermont, I bought some Pennsylvania maple syrup from the mountains of central Pennsylvania. It was impossibly different—dark, strong, rich! That was how we learned just how much real maple syrup was actually in commercial maple syrups. Most store-bought "pure" maple syrups are well over half corn syrup or cane syrup. What you buy in the mountains of central Pennsylvania, however, is pure, meaning uncut, maple syrup. If you taste it unawares, you're in for a shock. The store boughts, some of which have as much as 3% maple syrup in them, actually use imitation maple flavoring. So in the absence of real maple syrup, buy some imitation maple flavoring, like Mapleine, and make the following, which we call

Pennsylvania Maid Syrup

1 C water	2 C sugar*
½ tsp vanilla	½ tsp imitation maple flavoring**

*1 C white and 1 C brown sugar makes it nicer.
**Or forget the imitation maple flavoring and add to the above:
⅓ to ½ C pure Pennsylvania (uncut) maple syrup.

Bring the water to a boil. Add the sugar. When it returns to boiling, reduce the heat. Stir and cook for a few minutes at a gentle boil, until it is clear. Remove from the heat and add the vanilla and maple syrup or maple flavoring.

Croutons

Suppose bread crumbs, or even French Toast, is not to your liking (and you don't like to feed ducks.) What are you going to do with those pieces of stale bread? Cut those pieces of bread into little cubes. Into a nice heavy frying pan put a few tablespoons of olive oil. Then you can, but you don't have to, add some herbs to the oil. When the oil becomes fragrant, dump the bread squares into the hot oil and shake and stir to cook them until they start getting light brown. Just before you take them out of the pan, sprinkle Parmesan cheese over them, then some salt and pepper. They are croutons: for soups, salads, etc. They are as good and interesting as the bread from which you make them.

Bread Pudding

Let's go back to those halcyon days of our youth; back to a simpler time, free of the concerns that now too often sap the joys of our days. Let's do as we did then with impunity, and taste what is most probably the ambrosia supped on Olympian heights (no, not the subdivision, silly, I'm talking the real place). By the way, do not bake this in your bread machine! Yield: 2+ lbs of pudding.

3½ C milk	¼ C butter
⅓ to ½ C sugar	½ tsp salt
grated zest and juice of ½ lemon	3 C bread cubes
3 eggs	1 tsp vanilla
2 T Triple Sec or Grand Marnier	½ C raisins, chopped dates and/or pecans

1. Scald the milk, add the butter, sugar, salt, lemon zest and bread cubes, and let them soak in a large glass bowl.
2. Beat the eggs separately, adding the vanilla, lemon juice, and liqueur. Add the last to the former, gently stirring with a fork. Then stir in the fruit and nuts.
3. Place the bowl in a pan of hot water. Set this in a 350°F (177°C) oven and bake for about an hour and 15 minutes. Stick a knife in the middle. If it comes out clean, the pudding is done. Let it cool for a while; then eat it.

Index